LONELINESS
Symptoms and Social Causes

Barry W. Hancock
Albany State College
Albany, Georgia

UNIVERSITY
PRESS OF
AMERICA

LANHAM • NEW YORK • LONDON

Copyright © 1986 by

University Press of America,® Inc.

4720 Boston Way
Lanham, MD 20706

3 Henrietta Street
London WC2E 8LU England

All rights reserved

Printed in the United States of America

ISBN (Perfect): 0-8191-5639-6
ISBN (Cloth): 0-8191-5638-8

All University Press of America books are produced on acid-free
paper which exceeds the minimum standards set by the National
Historical Publications and Records Commission.

For Delores Ann, our families past and present . . .

. . . and for those that live their lives in quiet desperation.

ACKNOWLEDGEMENTS

I wish to extend thanks to Larry Perkins, Jack Bynum, and Ed Arquitt for their straightforwardness when reviewing this manuscript.

Anyone who is able to decipher my "chicken scratch" should be awarded an honorary degree in languages. With "honor", I thank Charlene Fries, Peggie Robinson, and for technical advice Marguerite Bonner.

TABLE OF CONTENTS

Chapter   Page

I.   AN OVERVIEW OF LONELINESS   1

II. THEORETICAL PERSPECTIVES   9
     Introduction   9
     Social-Cultural Perspectives   12

III. SOCIAL CHANGE AND LONELINESS ...   27
     Industrialization   33
     Bureaucratization   43
     Secularization   46
     Social Change and the Polarized
         Dialectic   53
     Summary   57

IV. A THEORETICAL TYPOLOGY AND
     DESCRIPTION OF LONELINESS   59
     The Bipolar Nature of Man   59
     Structurally-Situationally-Imposed
         Loneliness   63
     Structurally-Situationally-Imposed
         Loneliness and Social Institutions ...   70
     Structurally-Situationally Imposed
         Loneliness   79
     Other-Imposed Loneliness   81
     Summary   87

V.	THE THEORETICAL MODEL OF LONELINESS	91
	Interaction Within Component Impositions of Loneliness	93
	Locus of Control or Causality	94
	Stability of Polar Constructions of Reality	95
	Controllability of Selflessness	95
	Precipitation and Maintenance of Loneliness	97
VI.	CONCLUSIONS	99
	BIBLIOGRAPHY	103

LIST OF FIGURES

Figure		Page
1.	Reciprocal Social Interaction	13
2.	Static Asocial Directives	14
3.	Bureaucratic Asocial Directives	14
4.	Typologies of Societal Change	21
5.	Natural Dynamic Systems Compared to Unnatural Static Systems	43
6.	The Power Elite Policy-Making Process	51
7.	Dialectical Conflicts	54
8.	Dual Mental Constructs	55
9.	Ideal-Typic Dynamic of Social Action	61
10.	Present-Day Polarization of Social Action	62
11.	Social and Asocial Familial Structures	62
12.	Equidistant Adherence to All Reality Constructs and Placement of the Dual Generic Social Self	88
13.	Unequal Adherence by Imposition to Polarized Constructs and the Placement of the Asocial Fragmented Self	89
14.	Static Structural-Situational Impositions	92

PREFACE

Over the years the subject of loneliness has been discussed in self help books, poetry and with reference to the aged, newly divorced, and people receiving counseling. Somehow, loneliness is attributed to individuals who are unable to cope or are maladaptive. Though these areas are particularly problematic, the social change and institutions of a modern technological society have received proportionately less attention. It is as if the individual should constantly be responsible for coping and changing, (humans are "infinitely malleable" like molding clay) while the institutions of American society ever increasingly regulate and structure attitudes, belief, values, and behavior.

<u>Loneliness: Symptons and Social Causes</u>, attempts to focus primarily on conditions in society that are antecedent to the individual who exhibits symptoms of a greater social problems. For someone to feel lonely, alienated, powerless, and desolate <u>may not</u> be "abnormal" at all, given the conditions of American society today. To withdraw mentally and physical given these conditions may be one of the more sane endeavors in which we engage ourselves.

Albany State College Barry W. Hancock
Albany, Georgia

April, 1986

CHAPTER I

AN OVERVIEW OF LONELINESS

Why do I feel lonely? This is a question which has plagued human beings for milleniums of time. As we look through all recorded history and throughout civilizations past and present, we find philosophy, religion, and writings of many types (oriental philosophy, religion, the Bible, the Koran, Greek mythology, the writings of Shakespeare, Chaucer, and others), seeking to come to grips with this very basic human condition. Relatively speaking, the social sciences have undertaken very few investigations of loneliness, its causes, and genesis. Of the work that has been completed, much appears in self-help books and carries a compilation of testimonials from individuals who are asserting they have dealt with their loneliness. True as this may be, does this thorn in man's side have a different form and content for each person? Though loneliness is indeed a very personal phenomenon, are there general societal conditions which contribute to the felt loneliness of persons, and have these external circumstances magnified the intensity of that self-felt loneliness?

We want to begin by examining the problem, the questions, and what factors have contributed to such pervasive amounts of loneliness that exist in our modern world (Gordon, 1976). In the community of Toennies' (1957) gemeinshaft, small towns or neighborhoods had several strong relationships to affirm their self worth. Daily lives were reinforced and networks of contact were created. For instance, daily chores meant more than mailing a letter and shopping at a store. It was not a burdensome responsibility as much as it was various social events by which people gave one another mutual recognition. The butcher, baker, and constable were known as friends. Europe, in many areas, continues in this tradition, while America speeds ever ahead for efficiency (Gordon, 1976).

Loneliness, though a feeling common to all human beings, fluctuates with social change (Barrett, 1958; Fromm, 1955; Hammos, 1952; Laslett, 1960; Mills, 1956; Mumford, 1934; Simmel, 1950).

What may have been inevitable moments in a person's life can very quickly become a lifestyle for millions of people. Mass loneliness is not just a problem that can be dealt with by the particular individual involved; it is more an indication thta things are drastically amiss at the sociological level. When the societal is distinguished from the psychological, as noted by Jung (1955), an individual experience becomes a "collective disturbance."

Modern Western man does not seem to enjoy nor is he able to enjoy companionship, support, and protection from his neighbors. This is revealed in a community apathy and ambivalence towards the affairs of others. According to Gordon (1976),

> If someone walks out of a house with a TV set, a neighbor has no idea if it is the owner taking it t the repair shop or a burglar making off with an easy haul. You are not likely to enter into a spontaneous conversation on the street if you think the person addressing you is a potential mugger. We feel like strangers on our own streets. In a circular swing, more distrust and more loneliness. Where we should feel the safest, we rather feel that no one would help us if we were in trouble, that what happens to us, whether good or bad, makes no difference to the world around us--that we make no difference . . .(p. 19).

Many persons have been cut off from primary groups, family and kinship networks. Typically they live in an urban or suburban area where they meet people not as real persons but according to prescribed rules of conduct and modes of behavior. They work their whole lives, it seems, to obtain the newest comfort, convenience and fashion. In a mechanical industrial society, persons act primarily as consumers separated from direct and personal contact with the mental or manual creation of the consumed products. The lifestyle is one which centers on the acquisition of goods and control. Eventually as society has sought to control power, status, safety, and anxiety while maintaining a rationalized evolutionary order, Western man has found that he is unable to relate to his own nature and others, genuinely or authentically, slipping into a dread of nothingness. The inability to relate to nature and others has been the consequence of four centuries of development and change, where man as the subject has progressively increased his separation from the objective world (May, 1958).

Loneliness, though existent from man's beginnings, was once a philosophical problem of concern to poets and philosophers. Jeo-Christian religion expresses much of this concern in scripture written thousands of years ago (the King James Bible). Thomas Wolfe (1935) described loneliness in an essay with similar poetics:

> The hugh, dark wall of loneliness is around him now and he cannot escape. And the cancerous plant of memory is feeding at his entrails, recalling hundreds of forgotten faces and ten thousand vanished days, until life, until all life seems as strange and insubstantial as a dream. Time flows by him like a river, and he waits in his little room like a creature held captive by an evil spell. And he will hear, far off, the murmurous drone of the great earth, and feel that he has been forgotten, that his powers are wasting from him while the river flows, and that his life has come to nothing (p. 159).

Not only is loneliness a problem for the old and divorced, but for men and women in single bars, in encounter groups, adolescents running away from home or refusing to go to school, corporate executives, military personnel who move every few years, and others who keep crisis hot lines busy twenty-four hours daily.

Though loneliness knows no special class, race, or age of people that it affects, there are trends in the type of persons who are most likely to be lonely. A recent study from New York University concluded that the loneliness people are likely to be poor, uneducated, or minority groups, and unemployed. However, these external conditiions were not as strongly related to loneliness as a person's realization of the mismatch between their actual life and desired life (Rubenstein, Shaver, and Peplau, 1979).

An added dimension to loneliness seems to be that loneliness equals failure. Having people around us equals success. In this context, solitude is lonely; thus everyone should choose to have people around so they can be a success. The reasoning runs in this manner, so we engage in all types of events that will bring us in contact with people.

The association between failure, loneliness, and solitude is so strong in Western society that people often find it difficult to believe that there are people who actually enjoy being alone. Withdrawal from society by a person may receive harsh criticism by others, as if the person were "antisocial," a recluse, a "little strange." However, given the complexity of society and the ever increasing external constraints of the various institutions, withdrawal from society may be a sign of strength, not weakness (Gordon, 1976). To withdraw from society, in terms of solitude, is much more costly for many than to continue finding support from external sources, even though such sources may insure the loss of identity by submerging the self into group demands. These external conditions have not always been dominant to the exclusion of all else (Tillich, 1968). The modern society, described by Toennies as a gesellschaft, has removed the values of solitude and self-reflection by elevating a framework of positive law and rationality as the only valid mental construct. Kumar (1978) describes such a society and the shift to elevated rational constructs:

> Torn from the body of the organic community, the individual is thrown into large-scale associations to which, however, he has no right of membership . . . Social relationships are governed by the principles of rationality and calculation--especially economic rationality. Their typical expression is by contrast, arrived at a process of rational compromise among individuals each pursuing his own interest, and sanctioned by a framework of positive law (p. 91).

In addition to positive law and contractual agreements, we see the large city, the centralized nation state, and the work market. Though larger numbers of people are more densely gathered, they have lost their sense of belonging to a common social entity, owing to the contractual and instrumental nature of their relationships (Kumar, 1978). This separation of self from others and nature by the intervention of legal-rational systems (Weber, 1922) constitutes the primary condition of loneliness in modern society. The individual fulfills his role in order to attain a higher reward, not because there is intrinsic value in being one's self, but because there is an economic value toward which he is directed. However, when these external desired goals do not match the externally attained goals, the person is not left with any internal support or gratification. All seems to be lost; thus enters disparity. Feelings of being less than one ought to be, quickly forgetting that the rules for "being" are so often indoctrinated from an external, artificial, and economic base.

Because of the complexity of the emotions surrounding loneliness, its usage is often confused with other terms such as isolation, aloneness, alienation, and solitude. To be sure, these terms, by many, are used synonymously with each other in one terminological melting pot.

Loneliness, defined by Webster (1979), is a state of being lonely: (1) being without company; (2) cut off from others; (3) not frequented by human beings; desolate; (4) sad from being alone, lonesome; and (5) producing a feeling of bleakness or desolation. Already we can identify problems with such a definition, for these "definitions" may well be used for other concepts which are typically used synonymously with loneliness. Though loneliness shares characteristics with other emotional states, it must have unique qualities of its own, that is, a certain dynamic quality that sets it apart. If we can recall our own physical and emotional feelings of loneliness, we can usually remember a physical alteration. Some feel a pit in their stomachs; others experience loneliness as a sort of vertigo or a lack of color to life, a dulling of the senses. Other terms commonly used are empty, hollow, a vacuum. What begins to emerge is what we are talking about a feeling real or perceived by a given individual. Somehow we feel deprivation caused by the lack of contact with someone or something real, imagined, remembered, human, or metaphysical. Thus we have a dimension of past, present, and future, based on human contact and existential experiences. Whether the time dimension is based in realism (consumated time) or idealism (desired time) can affect the magnitude of felt loneliness. Usually both are present, as the two are not easily split except in a theoretical dialectic. By way of example, if we assume that most human beings are socialized, then we must also recognize that they are acutely aware of "supposed to be's" or "supposed to do's." Infants are supposed to have parents to give them food, protection, as well as love. Children are supposed to have parents and peers to love, and within them find companionship. As adults we are supposed to complete the social cycle with raising families in turn. Whether we speak of the family as a primary group or education, religion, and other numerous secondary institutions, we are acutely aware of the conflict that exists between the real and the ideal. As a person matures from childhood through adolescence, he/she moves out of primary support groups which emphasized cooperation, nurturance, and affective relations into the externally directed relations of competition. Such a structured existence places external constraints and prescribed modes of behavior on the person who has little or no input into determining what course of action is best for them.

Finally, we can describe <u>loneliness</u> as a feeling, real or perceived, of deprivation in social and intimate relations, with unfulfilled material expectations or existential feelings, resulting from the conflict between the real and ideal. Though this description covers the multidimensional nature of loneliness, we must be careful to point out that such parameters do not and cannot encompass the numerous behavior patterns of individuals as they deal with loneliness.

<u>Aloneness</u> is the objective condition of being by oneself. Although a person may be totally alone, this does not mean he/she feels lonely. Loneliness is the subjective feeling, while aloneness is an objective condition. However, usually people who experience loneliness also say they are alone, even in the presence of others.

<u>Isolation</u> is another objective condition of being by oneself. It is like aloneness but has an added dimension. Here detachment is stressed from others because of circumstances not under one's control. This may result from sickness, imprisonment, or certain types of natural disasters and accidents.

<u>Alienation</u> usually refers to certain perceptions individuals have about themselves and aspects of social environment. According to Urick (1970), alienation is characterized by five symptoms. These include social isolation (real or perceived), meaninglessness, normlessness, powerlessness, and self-estrangement. Man feels separated from himself and social others because of conditions external to himself. It is very difficult to speak of alienation in an absolute either-or sense. It is typified more accurately by degree and direction.

It is difficult to distinguish between alienation and loneliness, for these two terms may be applied to several of the same behavior patterns. However, the feeling with alienation and loneliness differs qualitatively. A person who is alienated may realize that he/she is powerless, leading a normless and meaningless existence, but may continue to seek soutions to the alienated feeling. For the lonely person, the feeling is more intense to the point of disability, hopelessness, desperation. Instead of feeling he/she does not belong to the social world and reconciling this position, the lonely person feels as if nothing can be reconciled. Thus we might think of loneliness as a specific form or subset of the broader, more general, category of alienation. The differentiation is then made by intensity and magnitude of the loss of self.

In that loneliness fluctuates with social change our primary concern will be to formulate a different way of thinking about loneliness which incorporates change and the idea of reality that we construct. A typology of the elements which affect loneliness must be examined and demonstrated by use of examples from existing literature, followed by suggestions for individual and social changes which must be considered.

C. Wright Mills (1969) referred to this as the "sociological imagination," that is, the ability to move with relative ease from specific social situations to large-scale social structures and societies and back again. With the sociological imagination, the microsociological settings of social interaction may be linked to macrosociological questions of class, power, and ethnic relations. To Mills, the sociological imagination makes possible an understanding of the larger society and the historical scene in terms of their meaning for a variety of individuals and an understanding of public issues. According to Mills (1959, p. 134), "it requires we avoid the arbitrary specialization of academic departments." Indeed, the following ideas by necessity must include topical areas from various disciplines to achieve a sociological imagination of loneliness (Cooley, 1966):

> I think, then, that the supreme aim of social science is to perceive the drama of life more adequately than can be done by ordinary observation. If it is to be objected that this is the task of the artist--a Shakespeare, a Goethe, or a Balzac-- rather than that of a scientist, I may answer that an undertaking so vast requires the cooperation of various sorts of synthetic minds: artists, scientists, philosophers, and men of action. Or I may say that the constructive part of science is, in truth, a form of art (p. 402-404).

Previous to the construction of a theoretical framework, our attempt will be to show, with sociological theories and a section concerning social change, why the felt loneliness of individuals stems not necessarily from personal maladaptation, but also from social institutions, societal complexities, and other external manipulations of the social world.

Specifically we shall examine changes in industrialization, bureaucratization, secularization, resulting alienation, and political ideologies that have deliberately detached man from himself and others for control. Thus we will take up these subjects as a backdrop to presenting a theoretical framework.

CHAPTER II

THEORETICAL PERSPECTIVES

Introduction

Though aloneness and loneliness are not the same, because of the differences in objective and subjective bases, respectively, there are presently more people living alone in the United States than ever before. According to the U.S. Census Bureau (1977), there was a 40 percent increase in "one person households" during a six-year period from 1970 to 1976 as there were in 1960. The indications of this report are that 15.5 million persons live alone in the United States, or 21 percent of all American households. Living alone does not necessarily mean that these individuals are lonely, but only that the physical conditions may be more conducive to feelings of loneliness.

The Census Bureau offers several suggestions as to why such a change has occurred. Marital dissolution has added to the number of people living alone. Young single persons and the elderly are more capable of financing separate households, particularly as apartment dwelling becomes more common. People are postponing marriage and children. When bearing children, the fertility rate is lower. In 1900, there were 4.8 persons per household as compared to 2.9 persons per household in 1976 (Glick and Norton, 1977).

Within the past decade, numerous self-help books have been published offering advice and numerous case studies in an effort to help lonely persons. Most notably, Moustakas (1961, 1972, 1975) discussed the benefits of loneliness as an integral part of becoming a total human being. However, though Moustakas mentions social elements as the creators of much emotional turmoil, he does not pursue much investigation into these problems. He instead seeks to give perscriptions of how persons may better cope with their circumstances in which they find themselves. This may be sufficient for a self-help book but does little in examining the etiology of loneliness. A transactional therapist, Eric Berne (1961), stressed "stroke" economies individuals may develop for themselves as a unit of recognition, structuring their time to receive the positive or negative reinforcement they need. Ira Tanner (1973), another transactional therapist, has suggested as a cause that loneliness is experienced by individuals because of their "fear of love." He blamed a lack of affection in childhood and suggested the "strokes" of affection and compassion as a panacea. Tanner (1973) explains:

> Our understand of loneliness depends mainly upon the perspective from which we view love. We see it usually from different vantage points:
> 'I don't deserve to be loved and I'll prove it.' I'm not O.K.--you're O.K. 'I don't trust people who want to give love and I'll prove it.' I'm O.K.--you're not O.K. 'I've given up trying to give love or receive it.' I'm not O.K.--you're not O.K. 'I try to give love and receive it.' I'm O.K.--you're O.K. p. 8.

Accordingly, the reason many persons never break away from loneliness is the insistence on making others responsible for our individual fears of love. Transactional therapists focus on the "Not O.K." feeling within the individual as one permanent emotion of an inferior personality. Feelings of inferiority, based on a fear of love, are a basic condition of childhood, leaving no one even in adulthood to escape loneliness (Mencken, 1963). Here again, we find no reference in transactional theories, Mencken to the external conditions and change that have brought about the increase in loneliness. This seems almost to say that loneliness is a problem of maladjusted persons who cannot cope, and the world about us is not responsible, leaving the cause for deficiency with the individual.

Viktor Frankl (1963), taking an existential approach to human problems, held that man is a spiritual being motivated not by the will to pleasure or the will to power, but by the will to meaning. Loneliness is a state of melancholia where persons become desensitized to the inherent values in their own being and subsequently to the values outside themselves. This increases to a point that persons view themselves, others, and life as meaningless. Guilt arises from feelings of insufficiency resulting in existential tension which in turn becomes eradicable guilt. Thus loneliness is seen as self-perpetuating. Howard (1975), also an existentialist, maintained that loneliness is inherent in the human condition, asserting the responsibility of each individual to find solutions for loneliness. Again we observe that no mention is made of external social factors as the producing forces of loneliness.

Gordon (1976) attempted to demonstrate through interviews the severe loneliness which is common particularly among the elderly and isolated persons in America. Several other attempts have been made in explaining peripheral aspects of loneliness while examining other problem areas. Zimbardo (1977) studied shyness. Caine (1974, 1978) studied the widowed. The timid and the assertive were studied by Bach and Goldberg (1975), and Bower and Bower (1976). Divorced and the newly single were examined by Hunt and Hunt (1977), Johnson (1977), and Wydro (1978). Not withstanding, the scanty research on loneliness specifically, studies on meaning in life, life satisfaction, and happiness have demonstrated that feelings of loneliness are pervasive (Lowenthal, 1964; Acuff and Allen, 1970; Hynson, 1970; Peppers and Knapp, 1980).

Theories such as transactional analysis, existentialism, and other psychological models fall into place as individualistic or dispositional perspectives of loneliness. The individualistic perspective seeks to ascertain what it is about a person that causes him/her to feel lonely in a given situation when others do not.

Sullivan (1953) maintained that loneliness was an inborn need for intimacy which arose if frustrated. If intimacy through the developmental stages of life is not present (with parents, peers, members of the opposite sex), loneliness will remain a critical problem.

Studies in ethological research maintain similar conclusions to that of Sullivan. Morris (1971) concluded that man through his evolution is a social animal, finding punishment when isolated for long periods of time. Bowlby (1973) asserted that humans through their evolution have developed a proximity mechanism based on the notion that it is safer for them to travel and live together. Being alone or feeling alone is a fear of human instinct. Fromm and Reichmann (1959) in a study of a psychiatric population pointed to a widespread fear of loneliness but maintained that "real" loneliness was found only in psychotics.

Thus, we can observe that individualistic theories of loneliness are diverse, basing the problem of loneliness on evolution or maladaptive patterns of behavior. Obviously, these theories only explain a part of the underlying condition affecting loneliness. However, it is necessary to at least make note of the work in the individualistic theories so that we may better understand the significance of social theories concerning this subject.

What emerges from the literature pertaining to loneliness can be generally separated into two categories: (1) the individualistic perspective including transactional analysis, psycho-analysis, evolution, and existential approaches in explaining loneliness; and (2) the social-cultural perspective which concentrates on the interaction of persons in groups and macro-level sociological factors. Primarily the main difference between the foregoing categorization would seem to be in the premise of causation. While the individualistic perspectives place the problem of loneliness within the individual as the source, the social-cultural perspective focuses on the external groups, organizations, institutions, and societal conditions that have been the source of felt loneliness in individuals. With regard to the present investigation, emphasis will be placed on the social-cultural as well as the subsequent theoretical framework.

Let us then proceed to review the sociological theories that have been applied to loneliness and related topics, as well as several perspectives that may apply but have not been utilized specifically for a discussion of loneliness.

Social-Cultural Perspectives

The social-cultural perspective focuses concern on the societal level of analysis as it pertains to the generation of loneliness in the individual. The author has chosen to include under this dimension cetain socio-psychological perspectives which, though previously have not been applied to loneliness in particular, are an integral part of the social-cultural perspective. Especially, this is the case when considering shared meanings and patterns of behavior reactions socially constructed.

The interactionist perspective of Mead (1918) emphasized the formation of the self. By understanding how the self is formed, we can hopefully draw upon some reasons for loneliness in humans. According to Mead, human behavior is not a matter of responding directly to the behavior. It is responding in such a manner that brings about the formation of the "self" (Meltzer, 1964). The self is the result of a social process within the individual involving two distinct parts-- the "I" and the "Me." The "I" is the impulsive, spontaneous, disorganized set of attitudes, definitions, and meanings common to the group. The "I" initiates the act while the "Me" gives direction to the act. As Mead

(1918) asserts:

> The 'I' or the ego is identical with the analytic or synthetic processes of cognition, which in conflicting situations reconstructs out of the protoplasmic states of consciousness both the empirical self (the 'me'), and the world of object. The objective world is a mental construct and is defined in terms of the needs of the 'I' of the ego. It is man's reply to his own talk. Such a me is not then projected and ejected into the bodies of other people to give them the breath of human life. It is rather an importation from the field of social objects into an amorphous, unorganized field of what we call inner experience. Through the organization of this object, the self, this material is itself organized and brought under the control of the individual in the form of so-called self consciousness (p. 401).

Thus the "I" offers the abilities for innovative, creative activity. The "Me," being regulatory, places on the individual the disposition to be socially goal-directed and conforming. Within the self, then, we have the basis for social control and novel behavior simultaneously.

Upon examining Mead's notion of "self" formation, he describes the interaction of the "I" and "Me" as a process. That is, a reciprocity of the inner drives and the outer constraints. Often those persons who say they are lonely describe their condition as a loss of identity, or in terms such as "I feel lost," and "I don't know who I am," or "What am I doing with my life?" Ideally, Mead's processes of social activity seem to apply best to societies which are less complex than those which the lonely person must deal with today (Figure 1). This author would

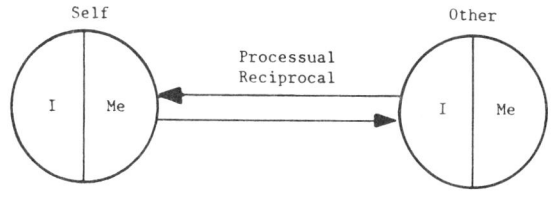

Figure 1. Reciprocal Social Interaction

concur with Mead that social relations should have a reciprocity for their existence. However, external structural constraints force a static relationship upon the individual's "me," denying a reciprocity of action of meaning to exist. Identity, meaning, and the self become externally constructed. The "I" is negated as external meaning in a rational scheme is seen as the only acceptable meaning. An ideal-typic rational scheme forces the imbalance of the self. The model in Figure 2 is used by way of illustration.

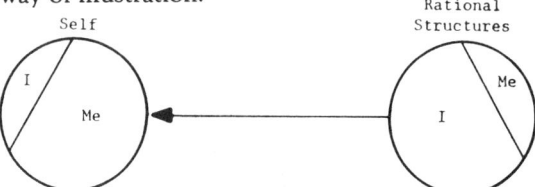

Figure 2. Static Asocial Directives

We see in Mead's "self" the opportunity for mutual input into a situation, its meaning, and outcome. This relationship we might find in a primary group setting of family or peers. But in a secondary rational structure such as institutions of education, religion, industry, and government, the "self" of Mead becomes something other than social, based on legal authority, power, wealth, and coercion. As we examine a bureaucratic structure, a whole series of patterns as the one just depicted begins to emerge.

Figure 3 represents the "Me" always as receiver of instructions, orders, or prescriptions, with the "I" as deflated and nonconsequential. The process of Mead's "self" no longer exists as a reciprocity, mutually derived, even though the meanings may be shared and the remnants of the "I" are existent. The legal rational structures have turned what was a process into a static mechanistic construct.

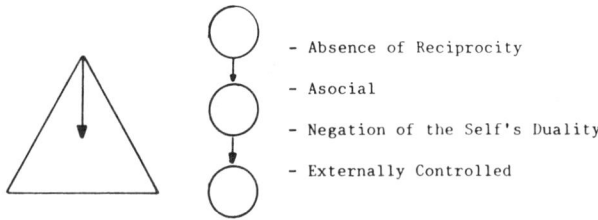

Figure 3. Bureaucratic Asocial Directives

According to Chapman (1972):

> Where the "I" aspects of the self are conditioned away and the contributions of 'I's' of the persons no longer have meaning, human values have been negated and lost. Where the remaining part of self, the conditioned 'me,' is reduced to a specific utility response of 'system needs' and nothing more, changing only as a system needs change, then for human beings mutilation has progressed so far that death becomes seductive and desirable (p. 30).

Though it may be argued that an individual has the prerogative to withstand external imputed demands of a nonsocial rational structure (Mead, 1912), we must also acknowledge the effects of socialization. Secondary, nonreciprocating socialization dominates the lives of individuals perpetuated by the parents and peers, who themselves have been and are being socialized by events and structures external to them. Most of our waking lives after about the age of a preschool child is spent in contact with some form of controlling institution.

Another interactionist perspective is that of Cooley (1902). Cooley asserted that human nature is social in content, consisting of three elements: the primary group, human nature, and the looking glass self. The individual is not only acquiring social standards but developing a self that reflects the definitions of society. At this level, individuals are extremely susceptible to social influences and control. According to Cooley (1902):

> As we see our face, figure and dress in the glass and are interested in them because they are ours, and pleased or otherwise with them according as they do or do not answer to what we should like them to be; so in imagination we perceive in another's mind some thought of our appearance, manners, aims, deeds, character, friends, and so on and are variously affected by it . . . The thing that moves us to pride or shame is not the mere mechanical reflection of ourselves, but an imputed sentiment, the imagined effect of this reflection upon another's mind (p. 36).

Thus, the self consists of the imagined expectancies and reflection of others the individual encounters. In reference to primary groups, Cooley (1902) characterizes these groups as intimate face-to-face associations and cooperation, describing the "we" fusion as sympathetic and mutual. These fusions between individuals create the unity where all have input. With regard to communities, Cooley (1902), like Toennies, characterizes them as:

> habits of free cooperation and discussion almost uninfluenced in the character of the state; and it is a familiar and well supported view that the village commune, self governing as regards local affairs are habituated to discussion, are a very widespread institution in settled communities, and the continuator of a similar autonomy previously existing in the clan . . . . In our own cities the crowded tenements and the general economic and social confusion have sorely wounded the family and neighborhood (p. 43).

The breakdown of primary social relations has found continuance in our society at the present time. The centralization of government and industry as we continue toward social "progress' has substituted secondary relations which are nonmutual and imposed this on the primary groups, traditional family group, and the community. Loneliness may then be seen as a breakdown of the community "we"-ness, where individuals now are forced to look out for number one that a competitive legal-rational society demands, disregarding the cooperative mutual trust that characterized primary groups. If man's primary social relations are destroyed, man will cease to be social, which undermines the survival functions of the family (Cooley, 1909).

Goffman (1959), with his dramaturgical approach, assumes the individual has an active role in determining the nature of the self. A key concept in this approach concerns impression management through the use of performances, props, and routines. According to Goffman (1959)

> The perspective employed in the report is that of the theatrical performance; the principles derived are dramaturgical ones. I shall consider the way in which the individual . . . presents himself and his activity to others, the way in which he guides and controls the impressions they form of him, and the kinds of things he may or may not do while sustaining his performance before them (p. xi).

We find Goffman viewing the individual as an actor on a stage, it would seem, in an inauthentic manner. True or real attitudes and beliefs of an individual can only be ascertained indirectly, never knowing with certainly what the latent motives may be. The content of any activity presented by an individual or the role it plays in an ongoing social process does not receive emphasis by Goffman, but the form the dramaturgical problem takes for the individual when presenting their activities before others. Many commentators have criticized Goffman for his conceptions of "humanity as the big con," the reduction of humanity to an act or performance, the "phony" element in all social performances, and man as a role player and manipulator of props, costumes, gestures, and words (Cuzort, 1969).

However, Goffman is criticized because his ideas of impression management, based on opportunists morals, are asocial in nature. These perspectives may fit well the society that has moved away from primary social gemeinschaft into a into a secondary self gain gesellschaft. Gouldner (1970), in commenting on Goffman's approach, points out that modern men and women are likely to be functionaries or clients of large-scale bureaucratic organizations over which they have little influence. Lacking this influence on organizational structure and its functions, they bend their efforts to the management of impressions that will maintain or enhance their status. Even values found in aesthetic standards have been reduced to the appearance of things (Gouldner, 1970).

Bittan (1973) believes such appearances have always played a part in social behavior, but never before has appearance been attached to aesthetics or in such a comprehensive fashion as in modern society. If values, morals, beauty, happiness, and meaning in life are but external appearances and acts, is it any wonder individuals feel empty, isolated in the presence of others, and alienated? Loneliness, it is held by several sociologists, is caused by the inherent alienation in modern society (Arendt, 1951; Fromm, 1955; Kenniston, 1960; and Seeman, 1975). The elderly, handicapped, racial minorities, and city dwellers are feeling powerless and their lives are meaningless, due to the crowding, urbanization, and separation from nature (Simmel, 1950). But loneliness is affecting not only these groups, though if well concealed in a performance as Goffman asserts, the loneliness may not be externally apparent. If loneliness is prevalent, why would an individual seek to conceal it, especially if he/she was aware of the social causes attached to the felt loneliness? Again we come back to America being a success-oriented society, highly competitive, and promoting of behavior based on only self-interest. Gordon (1976) suggests that Americans are encouraged to blame failure on themselves ("You can't cope;" "You're not able to adapt;" "You're weak"). Failure then carries a social stigmatization. To admit you are lonely is to admit social failure.

Reisman (1971) commented that Americans' expectations are too high based on the state of society. We want to be "cheerful," "happy," "successful," and "competent," but if we do not achieve these goals we suffer, not realizing that such goals are internally wrought. The industrial man, though, seeking to find what was once internally generated now turns to external sources. A shift has been made from internal striving to external controlling. Very much like the shift in Sorokin's (1971) swing from Ideational to Sensate forms of sociocultural change. Thus, shame and loneliness are associated, resulting in a "vicious circle of self-doubt and self-pity," as if to be lonely were some sort of un-American activity (Weiss, 1973).

In addition, the magnitude of the American political structures render to an individual feelings of being cut off from control and helpless (Kornhauser, 1959; and Nisbet, 1953). By the influence of external structures, the recent trend of "looking out for number one" has been advocated by professionals, clergy, mass media, and self help books as if to reassure people that they do have an internal locus of control in the midst of unchallengeable external influence. Thus, the paradox is revealed of desiring to maintain individualism but running the risk of becoming a social outcast. Or, conversely, adhering to the notions of progress, bureaucratization, and modernity to avoid condemnation, while at the same time losing a core identity by maintaining a continued imputed identity (Wolfe, 1976; Ringer, 1977; and Dyer, 1978). Ideally, we seek to do both; however, rarely can this be accomplished, for it is difficult to discern genuine activity from facades. Pirsig (1974) maintains that pure individualism is underconformity while the modern organizational man is an overconformist. We thus label them as psychotic or neurotic, respectively. Most fall on the continuum somewhere between these polarized states. Trying to maintain a middle position on the continuum, however, creates anxiety and frustration as well. According to Slater (1970), the needs of community, engagement, and dependence are frustrated by the commitment in America to individualism, competition, and independence; he admits "the competitive life is a lonely one." American role demands, at the same time, stimulate and frustrate needs which are basic to humans (Reisman, 1961; and Slater, 1970). The ethos of individuality and the insistence on competition inevitably generate alienation. Americans maintain the urge for a separate house, car, telephone, and television. The more we charge after privacy the more lonely we feel (Slater, 1970). People become a bother to us if we must break an institutional routine for social interactions. Bowman (1955) focused on social change as the dominant agent of loneliness. The primary group contacts have been severely reduced in frequency and intensity. Fearing autonomy and isolation, modern man has become compulsively conformist in an attempt to escape lonely feelings. This is derived from a powerless feeling, economically and politically (Fromm, 1941). This "compulsive conformity" is characterized by Reisman (1961) as a middle class America giving up autonomy and social freedom in order to gain approval in an individualistic and competitive society. The person who is overly conformist possesses a "false personalization" because of the inability to face the fear and loneliness of autonomy. False personalization appears to be very similar to Goffman's dramaturgical approach. We engage in overconformity, false impressions, and self-interest in order that we may be set with approval and rewards. Thus we are bound to an inauthentic secondary system of relations.

Reisman (1961), in <u>The Lonely Crowd</u>, has presented a discussion of loneliness, setting forth a typology of man as being "directed" in various ways as social-structural changes have occurred. These sources of direction include: (1) traditionally-directed, (2) inner-directed, and (3) outer-directed persons. These three types of social character are related to specific periods of time and cultural-historical change. Reisman views societies, particulary Western society, as moving through an S-shaped pattern of population growth. It is his thesis that each of the three different phases on the population curve appears to be occupied by a society that enforces conformity and molds social character in a definably different way.

The overriding character traits that a society possesses are seen to be affected by macro-level shifts in population size and the concurrent historical-cultural shifts that take place. Tradition-directed persons obtained a place in society by age-grade, clan, or caste. According to

Reisman (1961), such societies are roughly comparable to Europe before the Renaissance and seventh century. Innovative behavior or deviants were preserved by the important process of fitting them into existing roles such as a shaman or sorcerer. Society was aimed at survival because of the high mortality rates. Such a society based its lifestyle on folk, status, and geminschaft relations, characterized by a relatively slow change, dependence on family and kinship networks, and a fairly homogeneous web of values society wide. Allowances were made for the reciprocity of ideas, values, and beliefs encompassing a socially-derived consensus about issues.

A social structure imposing inner direction consists of increased personal mobility, rapid accumulation of capital, technological shifts, constant expansionism, colonialization, and imperialism. The source of direction for the individual is "inner," in the sense that it is implanted early in life by the elders and directed toward generalized, inescapable destined goals. Thus, inner-directed man receives more input to the self with little or no opportunity for reciprocity. Such a society presents its members with a great variety of aims--money, possessions, power, knowledge, fame; but such "aims" have not been socially derived as in a traditionally-directed society where survival tasks are dominant, as well as more of an equity between individual supply and demand, production and consumption. An inner-directed society finds its members having to constantly adapt to changes in technology, suffering from the "cultural lag" (Ogburn, 1922). The primary groups, family and peers, are loosened as well as the affective ties that are maintained by them. The affective ties become secondary as the shift is made to "other-directedness." Affective relations become validated by conformity to mass media stereotype modes of industrial efficiency, mass rationality or assumed rationality, where acceptable behavior is no longer socially bargained for but engineered for "systems maintenance" (Parsons, 1951). The other-directed individual has as his/her source of direction others upon whom he/she must depend for validation and, unlike the inner-directed person who is engaged in the acting, is acted upon. To illustrate Reisman's concepts of character types, consider the following diagram (Figure 4) presenting the related concepts of socio-cultural change.

Theorists	"Early" Society		"Modern" Society
D. Reisman	Tradition-Directed Society	Inner-Directed Society	Outer-Directed Society
H. Spencer	Military		Industrial
H. S. Maine	Status		Contract
F. Toennies	Gemeinschaft		Gesellschaft
E. Durkheim	Mechanical (Segmented)		Organic (Organized)
L. H. Morgan	Societas		Civitas
Levi-Bruhl	Prelogical		Logical
C.H. Cooley	Primary		Secondary
Sorokin and Zimmerman	Rural		Urban
H. Becker	Sacred		Secular
R. Redfield	Folk		Urban

Figure 4. Typologies of Societal Change (Lauer, 1973)

As noted in Figure 4, Reisman's theory resembles other theorists of social change, with the exception of adding the transitional category of inner-direction. The "false personification" spoken of by Reisman (1961) that is developed in modern society leads to widespread anomic patterns of thought and behavior. Children and adults are oversteered, maintaining super ego controls to the point of disallowance for normal satisfaction and the escape of other personality traits. This results in a sizeable number of Americans who exhibit clinical symptoms. What are these symptoms? Reisman (1961) compares post-World War II soldiers hospitalized for apathy with the modern widespread anomics:

> The most striking characteristics of the apathetic patient is his visible lack of emotion and drive. At first glace he may seem to be depressed; closer scrutiny, however, reveals lack of affect. He appears slowed up in the psychic and motor responses; he shows an emptiness of expression and a masklike face... They behave very well... complying with rules and regulations. They rarely complain and make no demands . . . (p. 244).

One need not look far to observe that such behavior is pervasive in America today. One must look only at others in restaurants, subways, night clubs, and any number of social gatherings. High conformity, in terms of clothing, etiquette, smiles, handshakes, and segregation by institutional status are present. But, as just described, one finds a lack of primary affect, lack of emotion and drive (except possibly when such would pay off in monetary or material gains), and mask-like faces. All of the external appearances of affluence and happiness are maintained while at the same time there is an internal loss of identity and emptiness. Silberman (1970) describes the paradoxical nature of this condition:

> ... economic growth reduces poverty, but it also produces congestion, noise, and pollution of the environment. Technological change widens the individual's range of choice and makes economic growth possible; it also dislocated workers from their jobs and their neighborhoods. Affluence plus new technology frees men from slavery to the struggle for existence, from the brutalizing labor that had been man's condition since Adam; it thereby forces them to confront the questions of life's meaning and purpose, even while it destroys the faith that once provided the answers (p. 145).

Finally, Reisman's character typologies are based on population trends that he posits are S-shaped and occur in all civilizations as they develop. In the latest preface of his book <u>The Lonely Crowd,</u> he modifies the population thesis as a determiner of the character types, though adheres to his typological scheme as indicative of societal development.

Park (1950), in his notion of marginal man, emphasizes that while an individual's personality has a physiological make-up, it achieves its final form under the individual concept of self. This conception is determined by the role which society assigns to him, and the attitudes others in society form of him. Thus, according to Park, self concept is a social product. The "marginal man" is a person considered not to be an ingroup or outgroup member. Park (1950) asserts:

> This personality type arises at a time and place where, out of conflict of races and culture, new societies, people, and cultures are coming into existence. The marginal man must live at the same time in two worlds culturally and socially. Inevitably, he becomes relatively to his culture milieu the individual with the wider horizon, the keener intelligence, and the more detached and rational viewpoint (p. 40).

However, it is also pointed out by Park that frequently the marginal man feels displaced and alienated as a result of his pseudo-cohesiveness to several groups. Because of the rapid changes in society, it would seem that many individuals are "marginal," increasing the feelings of loneliness and its perpetuation. If, because of rapid social change, individuals suffer from "cultural lag" (Ogburn, 1922), then nonmaterial culture--that is, internal values, meaning, and beliefs--are never changing quite as rapidly as the material culture. "Marginal man"-ness continues. Stonequist (1973) speaks of a culture duality facing the marginal man. His clash is not between inborn temperament and social expectations but between congenial personality tendencies and the patterns of a given culture. The problem is not adjusting to one self, but to several selves, that the role requirements of a society place on the individual. To harmonize these selves and integrate them so that meaningful inner life can be achieved is a problem. In a society of rapid social change where different codes of conduct exist, the difficulty of developing a meaningful existence is complicated as a function of rate of change. This can be the case for an immigrant to a new country, crossing racial boundaries, ideological changes in religion and politics, or by the crossing of boundaries with strong sectional traditions (such as move from a small town in West Virginia to the Watts area of Los Angeles, California). Such mobility is demanded of Americans today by industry for economic success. Social cohesiveness in primary groups is replaced with large groups of individuals who are marginal personalities. Stonequist (1937) admits:

One sees this dislocation clearly and sharply in the case of those individuals who fall between two major racial or cultural groups, but it is also apparent in the relations of groups such as social classes, religious sects, and communities. The individual who, through migration, education, marriage, or some other influence, leaves one social group or culture while making satisfactory adjustment to another finds himself on the margin of each but a member of neither (p. 22).

Such mobility as described above was studied by Packard (1972) in A Nation of Strangers. Geographic mobility deteriorates social networks, leaving only the mass communication network in which people must relate. Packard says this is the main cause of unhappiness, loneliness, and divorce in America. The average person in the United States moves 14 times, and 40 million persons change their addresses yearly. The result if a deprivation of a sense of identity (U.S. Census Bureau, 1977).

In addition to geographic mobility, cultural conflict plays a commanding role in the loss of identity. In a society where social classes are sharply defined, the upward mobility of an individual exposes them to social tension. (Summer (1906, p. 31) writes, "If a man passes from one social class to another, his acts show the contrast between the mores in which he finds himself." Strict conformity to rules regulations in industry may insure a promotion. If promoted, the person finds himself in a position now as boss over the persons who had formerly been contemporaries. The primary social interaction of peer to peer is broken down by the secondary institutional positioning. The person in this position suffers internal conflict, nevertheless conforms ever more ardently for job security, prestige and monetary rewards. If one continues to move upward in a pyramidal structure, the potential peer group continues to lessen. The author choses to term this "situational loneliness." That is, because of the secondary imposition of "codes for success" and the overconformity of the person, material success may be achieved, but identity in terms of close friends and primary interaction become less obtainable. The common expression, "it's lonely at the top," may be quite accurate in this sense. We must not think that only upward mobility can create loneliness for downward mobility or remaining in the same position in social structure can influence loneliness. Consider the 1960's when many youngsters were leaving middle and upper-middle class families to strive for a simpler existence. They created new subcultures and counter culture movements, because of the alienation they said had forced them to look for less materialistic values than what their parents espoused. But the loneliness of individualism affected them nonetheless. Those persons that remain stable in the movement within social strata see their peers and friends moving and shifting (or trying to) while they remain relatively stable. Again we see the paradox develop that upward mobility and geographic mobility may be sought to enhance economic gain, causing over-conformity. Those who seek downward mobility through alternative lifestyles, sub- and counter-cultures try to reject the dominant values of economic gain, thereby turning to individualism. Each end of the continuum finds loneliness a major factor in its effect.

Weiss (1973) has focused on disengagement theory as a descriptive model for loneliness. As society has increased in mobility and complexity, individuals are forced to constantly engage and disengage themselves from significant others. This may occur developmentally in terms of age and peer pressures, or formal positioning in a social strata such as a bureaucracy or geographic mobility. These constant shifts in structural definitions and boundaries reduce the chance for the longevity of relations with other persons. Weiss views loneliness as a relational deficit caused by either emotional or social isolation. The former reflects the absence of intimate relations with a parent, spouse, or lover, while the latter refers to the absence of involvement with a network of peers. Emotional isolation, the lack of an intimate tie, produces distress, driving restlessness, a re-experience of childhood abandonment anxiety, a "nameless" fear, and loneliness. Social isolation--the lack of a network of peer involvement--leads to boredom, feelings of exclusion, alienation, aimlessness, and loneliness. The distinction between emotional and social isolation can be difficult. Some have argued that emotional isolation is more accurately described as "desolation." That is, people who lose a close attachment are more likely to feel emotionally bothered and lonely more so than those who have never had one (Shanas, 1968; and Townsend, 1957). Being isolated is not axiomatic with being lonely.

Thus, we can observe that loneliness is a subject that has been investigated by several persons in the social sciences, alluded to by some, and equated with a variety of conditions in which man finds himself. Within the sociological perspectives, there appears to this author two areas which require investigation in more depth. The first of these is the concept of social change, as we have moved into modernity with notions of progress. The second is the recurring paradox of individualism as opposed to overconformity spoken of by Stonequist (1937), Fromm (1941), Nisbet (1953), Bowman (1955), Kornhauser (1959), Reisman (1961), Slater (1970), and Weiss (1973). What is it about social change in America that has produced such inner conflict in terms of identity and loneliness?

In this chapter we have sought to examine perspectives concerning loneliness. We have looked at psychological, social-psychological, and sociological investigations by several individuals. Some of the areas of review were specifically focused on loneliness while other areas were more general. What seemed to surface in the sociological perspectives concerning loneliness were two recurrent themes: social change and an individual's reaction to that change, consisting of a dilemma between individualism and overconformity to secondary institutional demands.

In Chapter III, we will investigate social change and loneliness more in depth, seeking to cast some insight on how loneliness developed into such a pervasive phenomenon. If we can discern where a breakdown in self-identity and loneliness occurred, it will then be possible to better typify loneliness and its dynamic as a framework for understanding present-day problems. Thus, we may generate future quantitative and qualitative research on the topic.

CHAPTER III

SOCIAL CHANGE AND LONELINESS

As we begin to trace the social change that occurred in the Western world, we shall begin during the feudal period in European history. The state as we know it today did not exist. Order was maintained on a personal and customary basis. The feudal (Gemeinschaft) attitude toward nature was one of passive conformity, accepting both the rewards and hardships of daily matters. Economic activity was judged according to need or use values, not by exchange or the market values of want (Rossides, 1978). The center of social being lay in tradition, either because it was of divine origin or because it had successfully withstood the test of time. The political order was maintained on a personal, customary basis. According to Rossides (1978):

> There was no impersonal, bureaucratic, civil and military administration, and no state organized on a legal-territorial basis with attributes of sovereignty. Feudal populations did not distinguish among law, custom, and morality, and they believed that the structure of intertwined norms in which they had their being had always existed as known at that time (p. 17).

Rather than a separation from nature characterized by a calculating egotistical reason, a collective sentiment existed. Social relations were seen in the family, the village, and the towns, or in the corporate organization of guilds, colleges, churches, and religious communities (Kumar, 1978). The basic organization of the Gemeinschaft was the family, which dominated ties of kinship, neighborhoods, friendship, and geographical location (Toennies, 1957).

Conversely, in the modern Gesellschaft society man is removed from the community organization, based on the family unit, and shifted into large-scale associations of which he is expected to give no more than a part of himself. Social relations are now, for many, governed by the principles of rationality (Kumar, 1978). This economic rationality now dominates the institutions of education, religion, and government in the Gesellschaft society of the present day, shifting morals and ethics into monetary policy. Self interest has replaced the community of the Gemeinschaft, leaving persons as isolates in an adversary relationship with others (Toennies, 1957).

Though persons in a Gesellschaft society are more densely gathered, Toennies (1957, p. 20) foresaw that "everybody is by himself and isolated." The sketch drawn of rationality based on self-interest is deeply rooted in the idea of liberalism which was pervasive during the enlightenment period. The ideas of the scientist and philosophers developed the notion that, by national progress and positivism, society could speed its evolution toward a Utopia.

With the enlightenment period, social philosophers sought to utilize the logic of Greeks as they pondered society. A fusion was made between Christian and Greek philosophies, particularly as the Roman Catholic church lost its dominant control in Europe. In The City of God, Saint Augustine, in the fifth century, by way of a philosophy of history and a theory of development, looked forward to the end of secular history as civilization moved from an earthly existence into a heavenly city. The "Golden Age" was seen to be always just ahead for Augustine, as well as for Kant and Saint-Simon 300 years later.

The sketch of the future was a society under the management of scientists and industrialists, speeding society toward the Utopian ideal. It was toward this Utopian ideal that society began to be engineered, as if scientific rationality and technology were the redeemers of social ills.

The philosophers of the time combined evolutionary theories of Darwin and Spencer with the religious Utopian ideal and the industrial progress ideas. It seemed every area of inquiry was seeking to determine how best to accelerate the attainment of bliss. One cannot criticize the thought of creating a world of harmony and order. However, the means for achieving such a world were imbued with rational constructions of thought, institutions, and bureaucracy, which could not and have not accounted for the bipolarity of reality construction--namely, those aspects which are irrational, spontaneous, and impulsive. Novel behavior and change do not fit well into a "rational" construction of society.

Scientific reasoning and calculation would be applied to all problems of values and ethics, so that social conflicts could be resolved by appeal to criteria which were universally accepted. Weber (1922), though he maintained that society would finalize itself in legal-rational bureaucracy, surprisingly issued a grim vision:

> Together with the machine, the bureaucratic organization is engaged in building the houses of bondage of the future, in which perhaps men will one day be like peasants in the ancient Egyptian State, acquiescent and powerless, while a purely technical good, that is rational, official administration and provision becomes the sole, final value, which sovereignly decides the direction of their affairs (p. 56).

He adds:

> This passion for bureaucracy is enough to drive one to despair. It is as if in politics wewere deliberately to become men who need 'order' and nothing but order, become nervous and cowardly if for one moment this order wavers, and helpless if they are torn away from their total incorporation in it. That the world should know no men but these; it is in such an evolution that we are already caught up, and the great questions is, therefore, not how we can promote and hasten it, but what can we oppose to this machinery in order to keep a portion of mankind free from this parcelling-out of the soul, from this supreme mastery of the bureaucratic way of life (Weber, 1922, p. 57).

The great appeal of Utopian progress was the possibility of eliminating chance and capriciousness in human life. By using logic and pure reason, science could eliminate not only physical prolems of disease and plague but could also engineer social concerns into a rational scheme. By joining physical science with social philosophy, a new era of "social physics" could emerge (Comte, 1830). Ideally, social prescriptions were to be made by the experts, men of knowledge, engineers, mathematicians, and economists. Bankers and industrialists would conduct their affairs without bias or political position, basing their decisions on the new society. The difference seems to be in what or who has dominated. Personal dominance by a king or lord has been replaced by dependence on an objective order of things which is generated by a "higher" rationality. The constraints of life are to live and die rationally and productively. However, the Utopian ideal and the constructed apparatus for achieving that ideal defeated its own purpose to create a humane existence. By the technical utilization of persons as "things," the struggle for existence became more scientific and rational. While scientific management and divisions of labor increased productivity in nearly all reas including the standard of living, the patterns of behavior and the mind revealed critical problems and oppression. Increasing the role of capital destroyed the medieval social system, removing the individual from a relatively stable community relationship (Fromm, 1941).

The paradox for the individual under such circumstances was freedom from the bondage of economic and political ties while simultaneously being freed from the ties which used to give him security and a feeling of belonging. The relationship between persons was greatly altered as they moved away from these ties of security and belonging (Fromm, 1921):

> His relationship to his fellow men, with everyone as potential competitor, has become hostile and estranged; he is free-- that is, he is alone, isolated, threatened from all sides... and helplessness... The new freedom is bound to create a deep feeling of insecurity, powerlessness, doubt, aloneness, and anxiety (pp. 80-81).

The image of evolutionary progress toward a Utopia held by social philosophers of the 18th century sought to obtain a "paradise" by objectification and a rationalizing of the social order. However, the attempt to totally rationalize every aspect of man's existence became immensely irrational with respect to the internal meaning, identity, and loneliness. Today it seems that every area of life is being quantified and in so doing we believe we have arrived at an explanation of a given phenomenon.

Applications of mathematical structures, nomenclature, and symbols may provide an aid to describing a certain event, but this does not explain that event. For example, we may choose to "describe" a human sex cell with component protoplasm, mitochondria, flagella, and ribonucleicacid (RNA). We may "describe" chromosomal patterns and genetic structure. However, is it ultimately possible to "explain" why a microscopic cell division, when given time to develop, grows into a human being who is the same but different than all other living creatures? Typically, a scientific, rational description consists of a linear chair of events, each given a special name or symbol. The problem arises when the symbol is taken to be the total explanation of the real. The present society takes symbols to be real and acts accordingly. If we assume bipolarity of man and human beings as dynamic, then reality is not explained by symbols which are static devices of description. It is misleading to think that description is explanation, yet modern society has been led to do just that. Replacement of the authentic, dynamic, bipolar understanding has been successfully achieved with the inauthentic, static, polarized modes of control. It is in this type of existence that we find lonely people hammered into a statically constructed "reality" for the maintenance of order. What is objective and empirically verifiable has become for many the truly valid construction of reality. A society of people becomes extremely predictable and controllable when their irrational subjectives selves are negated. Appeals to a high loyalty, tradition, aesthetics, and deeply religious orientations become the focus of castigation. Such beliefs are a threat to those who would maintain power, for the persons engaged in unconventional thought and belief are less likely to be controlled.

Thus, the past and the present are not particularly important in the progression toward Utopia. What is important is prediction and control. Given the dynamic nature of man, prediction is not well accomplished unless we control man first and then predict. Technological society has not left man as the controller but as the controlled. Carlyle (1829) believes:

> Not the external and physical alone is now managed by machinery, but the internal and the spiritual also ... The same habit regulates not our modes of action alone, but our modes of thought and feeling. Men are grown mechanical in head and heart, as well as in hand ... Their whole efforts, attachments, opinions, turn on mechanism, and are of a mechanical character ... Mechanism has now struck its root down into man's most intimate, primary sources of conviction; and is thence sending up, over his whole life and activity, innumerable stems--fruit bearing and poison bearing (pp. 65-67).

Paul Tillich (1953) sought to elaborate on persons in a technical society and their inner struggle against depersonalization. He describes the existential approaches of Kierkegaard, Neitzche, and Sortie, as they discuss the bipolar nature of man. If we consider meaninglessness, powerlessness, and normlessness as characteristics of the alienated and lonely person, how has modern society created these feelings with the individual? Let us, by way of example, take the concepts of beauty and ugliness. These concepts are relative in their relationship. That is, what we consider as beauty is beauty only as a mental construct. Can something be said to be inherently beautiful or ugly? What is beautiful, good, and righteous to one person may be ugly, evil and sinful to another. Nonetheless, man develops agreement realities with others, a consensus as it were, about beauty or any other numerous constructs.

However, agreement reality between persons consists of an exchange or reciprocity of ideas subjective and objective in nature. The concept of happiness, like beauty, is derived likewise. In modern society something has gone amiss. Beauty and happiness are defined not socially through consensual reciprocity but are defined through objectification. Such comments as "if I only lived somewhere else," "if I only had more money, then I'd be happy," "happiness is a new car," "beauty is designer jeans, Max Factor makeup," and so on suggest that the concept of success for most is monetary gain. A shift has occurred in the locus of meaning from mentally socially-derived constructs, consensual in nature, to engineered constructs which have their locus of meaning external to the individual. Can we avoid a meaningless, lonely existence if our sense of identity and meanings are objectified and rational? If meaning in life is placed in material goods, have we not polarized our very own dynamic nature, negating or ignoring the alternative pole in the dialectic of subjective experience and spiritual or nonmaterial existence? There is irrationality in rationally seeking to progress to a Utopia by polarized objectivity. It is from this standpoint that social change is so crucial in the consideration of loneliness. Reich (1970) comments on the polarization engineered by a "corporate state" and the effects on persons:

> They work under terrible stress, which prevents them from finding more genuine meaning and is likely to drive them to ulcers, heart attacks, or the psychiatrist's coach. In Marx's sense, they are alienated from their determinate selves, alienated from their work, and alienated from their needs...
> Many have several different and separate selves, different roles which are not integrated and prevent anyone from confronting the individual as whole. They have surrounded

themselves by things, and rendered themselves passive in the process; it is as if they have given up the power to change and grow and create, and things have acquired this power instead; things change and dance and the individual sits motionless, besotted, and empty . . .

. . . The productive state has demanded output from them all their lives, draining them of life, creativity, vitality, and never giving them a chance to be renewed. Competition has made them fearful and suspicious of their fellow man, believing that every other man is not a brother but a threatening rival with a knife at the throat of his adversaries. Imprisoned in masks, they endure an unutterable loneliness (p. 165).

Man of modern society is driven by an external, objectified, rational authority. Caring little about their work or uncognizant of their social conditions, modern man exhibits a hollow social death. The hierarchial structure of the productive state imposes a low esteem on the individual as systems material. Such impositions create a working force for the machinery of the state and create a condition of inferiority in which the individual is looked down upon by society and looks down upon himself because, as Reich (1970, p. 145) asserts, he is "not as good as someone more successful." There has been a shift in values of beauty, happiness, success, and satisfaction from social agreement consisting of internal and external influences to an increase in external asocial directives which are marketed.

After consideration of the development and change that has taken place, the conditions of society that are conducive to widespread loneliness can be identified descriptively. Important to this description is the duality of man's existence. If the duality of the dialetic, objective-subjective components is denied or polarized (in this case, objectified), can there be anything but a meaningless, lonely existence? Let us proceed to examine specific areas of modern society, their change, development, and the duality denial to persons that they impose.

Industrialization

It would seem at the center of industrialization there lies a series of economic changes, and that the merit of such changes are indicated by the growth or progess of the economy. However, what is also involved in industrialization is a vast number of social changes. Associated with this change are specific components of the industrial system. Major and constantly changing technology means more work is done by machines rather than by hand. People's labor is marketed. Work is concentrated in single enterprises. A new social type emerges, that of entrepreneur (Burns, 1969). Such change has brought about urbanization, incraesed mobility, rationalization, secularization, and bureaucratization. To become industrialized is supposedly to become rational. The process has affected not only public places and work, but relations of family, marriage, and personal friendship.

If we examine the major social institutions of family, religion, education, government, and industry, we find that a dramatic change has occurred in their interrelationships. The family was once primary in its role for survival. The other institutions, particularly government and industry, were created as secondary agencies to be used as tools for the insurance of familial survival. Such institutions were designed and operated by families, for the cooperation and consensus on group policy was critical for survival. There were arguments, disagreements, and resolvement. The interaction was socially dynamic. In today's society we find that this dynamic has been replaced in the legal-rational systems by a static order. All of the major institutions have an asocial character to them by inducing chains of rational command based on persuasion, command, or coercion. The one remaining group that still maintains a somewhat social character is the family, but even the family is breaking down because of the rigid structured inability of persons to maintain reciprocal social relations. How can persons maintain genuine social relations when the society they live in has stripped them of input and all other areas of life have been quantified, rationalized, and bureaucratized.

The basic survival group, the family, that once created the other institutions of religion, education, industry, and government to help insure its survival, is now threatened. These secondary institutions have been so dominant as to diminish the primary family group that first created them. Through a process of urbanization, industrialization, and consequential increases in mobility, the family has decreased from an extended type to a nuclear family, moving presently to a great number of single-parent families. It would seem that secondary institutions set in rationalism have become of primary concern, while the family and social interaction between persons has become of secondary importance. It is almost as if it would behoove us to keep the family organized socially, in order to insure the survival of the rational, institutional structures. The continued focus on utopic progress is adversely affecting the family and individuals as they find interacting authentically more difficult. They are becoming victims of a move much past survival structures based on "need," to domination, competition, power, and exploitation based on "want." Slater (1970) comments:

> We talk of technology as the servant of man, but it is a servant that now dominates the household, too powerful to fire, upon whom everyone is helplessly dependent . . . We never ask, for example, if the trivial conveniences offered by the automobile could really offset the calamitous disruption and depersonalization of our lives that it brought about. We simply say 'You can't stop progress' and shuffle back inside (p. 25).

While industry has been able to far surpass the material needs for survival by offering a wide array of material wants, society and social beings have paid the price. Rational efficiency and organization are very effective in producing materials; however, the competition, automation, rigidity present do not produce the psychological (internal) needs of the person.

Industrial society by focusing on quantity of production, quantity of labor and output, and the quantification of humans has overlooked the quality of the product, quality of work conditions, and the quality of morale. In recent years we have experienced a lessening of the ability to produce and compete with other nations that haven't forgotten quality work. If there continues to be a little pride in work, because of work conditions and remuneration, we will continue to produce junk wrapped in a pretty package (i.e. automobiles, appliances, housing). Individuals must have internal as well as external needs fulfilled. We are out of balance when only the external wants are sought. Furthermore, not only are the internal needs lacking, they are depleted.

> We seek a private house, a private means of transportation, a private garden, a private laundry, self-service stores, and do-it-youself skills of every kind. An enormous technology seems to have set itself the task of making it unnecessary for

human being ever to ask anything of another in the course of going about his or her daily business. Even within the family Americans are unique in their feeling that each member should have a separate room, and even a separate telephone, television, and car when economically possible. We feel more and more alienated and lonely when we get it (Slater, 1970, p. 13).

Capitalism, communism, imperialism, or whatever label we give to rational power structures has little significance, except to create in-group/out-group cohesion mechanisms as a rationale for more industrialization and military spending. Far from solving man's basic internal needs alienation and loneliness are immeasurably worsened. In liberating man from social responsibility based on values and ethics contained internally, the external succeeds in creating deep feelings of insecurity, powerlessness, doubt, loneliness, and anxiety (Fromm, 1941). Rational structures of industry, which disallow the duality of man, condemns the worker to experience himself not as a person but as a commodity or object to be traded, bought, and sold. The move away from craftsmen to specialized functionaries has meant that while rational efficiency is sought, persons are removed from the creative aspects of producing a "whole" product containing personal characteristics of name and design. Quality is negated in the name of quantity.

> What is the modern man's relationship of his fellow man? It is one between two abstractions, two living machines, who use each other. The employer uses the ones he employs; the salesman uses his customers ... There is not much love or hate to be found in human relations of our day. There is, rather a superficial fairness, but behind that surface is distance and indifference (Fromm, 1941, p. 60).

This specialization of task prevents persons from having any vested interest in artfully producing a "whole" product which will bear their name and reputation. Not only are tasks specialized but so too are knowledge and the flow of information, as labor is divided and arranged in an economic and status hierarchy.

For Karl Marx, the division of labor was central to the process of capitalist industrialization. According to Marx, this division, while existing in all societies throughout history, underwent an immense qualitative change under a capitalistic orientation (Marx, 1867). The crucial distinction of the division of labor systems was in the authority exercised over the worker. The social division of labor saw independent producers coming together buying and exchanging commodities among themselves, subject to free competition. The industrialized division of labor implied an absolute and despotic authority of the capitalist over the workers. Industrialization encases a decisive separation of a knowledgeable management from a knowledge-less work force, a conception from execution, of mental from manual labor, and the artisans' loss of the instruments of independent production, socially maintained. Industrialization has had the effect of objectifying workers and their work; quality work for the love of craftsmanship and personal self esteem (Kumar, 1979).

In the present historical situation, under capitalism our essential being is deprived--the separation of existence and essence in the tragic condition of human life in a capitalistic society (Quinney, 1980). The contemporary capitalistic world is caught in what Paul Tillich--going beyond Marx s materialistic analysis of capitalism--calls a sacred void, the human predicament on both a spiritual and a socio-political level (Tillich, 1948).

The effects of capitalistic industrialization on the loneliness of the individual are apparent in the systematic separation of man from his nature. Quinney (1980) concurs:

> Among the various characteristics of present civilization are a mode of production that enslaves workers, an analytic rationalism that saps the vital forces of life and transforms all things (including human beings) into objects of calculation and control, a loss of feeling for the translucence of nature and the sense of history, a demotion of our world to a mere environment, a secularized humanism that cuts us off from our creative sources, a demonic quality to our political state, and a hopelessness about the future (p. 3).

Distance and indifference are found in social interaction, but the competition and mistrust imposed by the industrial/economic system is widely apparent. What are the characteristics of orgnaization people or the industrial man?

Whyte (1956) has given an in-depth appraisal of the "orgnaization man." The paradox of the individual versus the collective good is apparent in the corporate philosophy. Officially, Americans espouse the Protestant ethic, that is, the pursuit of individual salvation through hard work, thrift, and competitive struggle. Individualism of personal responsibility for gain is the current rhetoric. Corporate man evangelizes individualism while at the same time does not realize that the very corporation vested in rational power structures is preventing everything except a myopic individualism. Corporations are asocially derived collectives. To suggest that industry and corporations are imposed viciously as collectives for control is not conceivable to the corporate executive, though he is engaged in a collective which is more detrimental to individualism than any organization he may warn against as being subversive. William Whyte (1956) observes:

> Collectivism? He abhors it, and when he makes his ritualistic attack on Welfare Statism, it is in terms of a Protestant Ethic undefiled by change--the sacredness of property, the enervating effect of security, the virtues of thrift, of hard work, and independence. Thanks be, he says, that there are some people left--e.g. businessmen--to defend the American Dream . . . Only by using the language of individualism to describe the collective can he stave off the thought that he himself is in a collective as pervading as any ever dreamed of by the reformers, the intellectuals, and the utopian visionaries he so regularly warns against (p. 6).

The essence of the corporate man and the created state is a single homogeneous mind. He has only one mind, one value: the value of technology, organization, efficiency, growth, and progress. Control and direction of most everything has been turned over to corporate orientations--the natural environment, our lives, our minds (Whyte, 1956; Reich, 1970; and Quinney, 1980).

Happiness is a commodity as well as success, love, beauty, and most other subjective experiences and values. The idea of administration is that the best way to conduct activity is the rational control of that activity. The random, irrational, and alternative ways of doing things are banished. The lonely feelings of emptiness, being out of self-control, and loss of identity are not terribly misunderstood if we observe these daily modes of corporate control. It seems endemic that the loss of identity leads to escapism in which we seek to regain those aspects of ourselves which are creative, spontaneous, and irrational. Escapism then is a compensatory activity against the objective-rational imposition of a corporate, bureaucratic structure. Quinney (1980) states:

> True human nature is impossible under the conditions of capitalism, and true humanity can be achieved only in a protest against this estrangement. Human physical existence must be vitalized, and spiritual and social life must be restored. The ontology of being, in fact, moves us to continually inquire into the meaning of our social existence and to question the estrangement of this existence from our essential being (p. 4).

Through the overrationalization within corporate structures maintained by the major social institutions, it is impossible to close the separation between existence and essence or create a reality in which a human "wholeness" is more fully realized (Quinney, 1980). It is not unusual that more individuals are finding escape necessary.

There has been a recent shift in the move back to rural areas in terms of vacation places and a second house. That is, families are working in metropolitan area, then traveling during "time off" to less dense areas for recreation. This move is predominantly characteristic of the more affluent who maintain employment in an urban, industrial, area while maintaining a weekend or summer retreat. But if one has not the means to leave the metropolitan area, the need to escape is still present. Drug use is prevalent in all areas and social classes. The use of amphetamines and barbiturates, with the accompanying addiction, are the most used drugs in America. The addicts tend to be middle and upper class professionals (Hill, 1976). If we consider the alcohol, caffeine, and tobacco use, drug usage is alarming at all social class levels.

But is it the drug use that is the problem or the need to escape from an overly rationalized life? If we are affluent, we may have a boat, an airplane, or a place in the country for weekends including a fully stocked bar. If we are not so affluent, we may have a six pack of beer, a "joint" of marijuana, or various pharmaceutical means of escape in the mind without a change of surroundings. To drastically change one's surroundings for the purpose of escape is costly. We see that both legal and illegal activities, as well as socially accepted or rejected behaviors, are not the issue nor is the increased policing of activity. More law enforcement in society means only more lower class individuals are arrested, given ineffective court appointed attorney and then convicted. The upper class individual remains anonymous by being able to move and cover any illicit activities in which they may be engaged. Having the money and time they are defended successfully out of the grasp of the court. Even justice has become a commodity to be bought and sold. How one escapes and how they are treated when illegal activities are detected is a significant question of social class. What becomes the major issue nonetheless is the increasing need of persons at all social class levels to escape from their daily overstructured existence.

The mode of escape, it would seem, is dependent on our economic status. Has corporate rationalism had a determining role in the loss of identity? Reich (1970) provides us with an in-depth analysis of the corporate state, explaining the modern society of objectified rationalism is:

> a society which is entirely indifferent to human needs and values, which can be wholly irrational, which can indeed make distructive war on its own people. What medium could possibly furnish a way for human needs to emerge so distorted and ignored and yet keep the people believing that it was 'their' society?. . . Law is such a medium. . . that is capable of being wholly external to the self. . . When law is employed to serve the Corporate State, the people do not know what has been done to them for law gets into the individual's mind and substitutes its external standards, whatever they may be, for the individual's own standards (p. 138).

The control in the corporate state is not as much a matter of consensus versus conflict as it is controlling every waking hour with rigid rationality. The greater the number of laws the greater the resulting discretion, and the more lawless the official part of the state becomes. Yet we have more laws not to control crime but to maintain the illusion of rationality in a state that is irrational in its control. How can it be rational when it disallows a whole series of diverse, "apparent," irrational behaviors that are socially constructed or are a reaction to rational constraints which have not been socially derived?

In a society which is based on rational constructs disallowing human duality, we are confronted with industry and technology wearing the robes of egotistical godhood. That is, the environment to which man is an integral part has become not a cooperative system for survival but an engineered exploited entity for man's insatiable competitive wants. Here the reciprocity has been lost, and a power relationship of man's technology and industry seeks to rationally control the environment. The power control for profit has extended into this area no less than every other aspect of man's existence. But what happens when we separate man from his nature, controlling every aspect of his physical surroundings? The problems of identity and loneliness are likely to occur. We have created for man a lifestyle of objective sterility. Even the dislike for nature in general becomes apparent. As long as the problems of our existence in relation to nature are removed from our immediate field of vision, we assume they do not exist. Slater (1970) calls this the "Toilet Assumption." Rational structures have the notion that the unwanted matter, unwanted difficulties, complexities, and obstacles will disappear if they are removed from sight. Consider prisons, the aged, the mentally disturbed, or the infirm. If we keep these people out of sight, our rational structure can maintain its control for the irrationality will not be detected. Slater (1970) explains:

> We don't connect the trash we throw from the car window with the trash in our streets, and we assume that replacing old buildings with new expensive ones will alleviate poverty in the slums . . . The result of our social efforts has been to remove the underlying problems of our society farther from daily experiences and daily consciousness, and hence, to decrease, in the mass of population, the knowledge, skill, and motivation to deal with them (pp. 21-22).

Here we see the separation that exists between man as producer and consumer, responsible for his own waste, cooperating with the ecology that supports him and finding meaning in a natural environment. To cooperate with nature goes against the precepts of a rational control, for this control must be one-sided, profit seeking, and competitive. Hardin (1968) explains the result of a rationalized, competitive system on the environment in an essay entitled "The Tragedy of the Commons." Because each individual desires to better their life situation in terms of material goods, they continue to consume more and more of the earth's resources. The problem is that if each person, being "rational," seeks to maximize his/her gain simultaneously without limit, the limited resources of the earth will be depleted, thus destroying life. An economic system that is based on the freedom of maximum gain for all will bring "tragedy to all" (Hardin, 1968). This rational orientation disallows the cooperative, reciprocating, duality in nature, compounding the problem of denying the duality to exist man's mind. Instead of giving back to nature in equal proportion that which we take, we competitively take resources (maximize gains) and reimburse nature with little or nothing (minimize costs).

If the static rationalism of control does not begin to strive for a more equal position of dynamics, the consequence is destruction of the very life support system. Rodale (1972) has maintained that the rational man-made system is overly simplified and not self-sustaining (Figure 5). How can they be? Profit and control for power do not permit it. Profit can only be had by taking more and giving less. In reciprocal relations which take into account the duality of nature, each participant in an interaction gain and lose by interdependency (dynamics). To maintain a rational order, one participant must be dependent while the participant in the power position commands. Leopold (1949) discussed this concept:

> There is as yet not ethic dealing with man's relation to land, and to the animals and plants which grow upon it. Land, like Odysseus's slave-girls, is still property. The land relation is still strictly economic, entailing privileges but not obligations (p. 201).

The ecological problems that have become existent as man has been separated from nature, as well as the escapism previously discussed, are the by-products of industrial and technological manipulations. The by-products, and they are many, are the symptoms of the overrationalization of social life. It becomes apparent that a rational progress toward Utopia is terribly irrational, especially if the progress is destroying the very systems that support it. The social bond, primary reciprocal relations, and the environment (dynamic relationships) are negated.

Dynamic	Static
Natural Ecosystem: Pond, Marsh, Grassland, Forest, Etc.	Man-Made System: House (Conventional), Factor, Parking Lots, Etc.
1. Captures, converts, and stores energy from the sun.	1. Consumes energy from fossil or nuclear fuels.
2. Produces oxygen and consumes carbon dioxide.	2. Consumes oxygen and produces carbon dioxide.
3. Produces carbohydrates and proteins; accomplishes organic synthesis.	3. Cannot accomplish organic synthesis; produces only chemical degradation.
4. Filters and detoxifies pollutants and waste products.	4. Produces waste materials which must be treated elsewhere.
5. Is capable of self-maintenance and renewal.	5. Is not capable of self-maintenance and renewal.
6. Maintains silence.	6. Usually creates noise.
7. Maintains beauty if not excessively disturbed.	7. Usually causes unsightly deterioration if not properly engineered and maintained.
8. Creates rich soil.	8. Destroys soil.
9. Stores and purifies water.	9. Often contributes to water pollution and loss.
10. Provides wildlife habitat.	10. Destroys wildlife habitat.

Figure 5. Natural Dynamic Systems Compared to Unnatural Static Systems (Rodale, 1972)

Bureaucratization

The mechanism of the rational philosophy which enforces the control and subsequent duality breakdown in individuals is bureaucracy. We previously discussed the characteristics of the legal-rational system (Weber, 1922) in our section on industrial change and the separation of man's duality. Let us discuss more specifically the characteristics of the power structure that has radically altered government, industry, education, religion, and most importantly, the family. It is the position of this author that alienation, identity problems, and loneliness have become pervasive as rational systems continue to disallow man's irrational subjective experience of himself. There is no profit in this nor is control, externally imposed, a viable mechanism of power. Urban areas which are characterized by specialization through rational legitimized rule have developed "specialized" knowledge. But the price of this increase in specialization is a breakdown in social communication.

Complex differentiation, specialization of knowledge, and work diminish the possibilities for enlightened communication among the generally educated. Conversation becomes a lost art, diminishing the prospect of spiritual community (Roszak, 1973).

This is not unlike the Biblical story of the Tower of Babel. According to this story a tower was constructed using the greatest technology and organization that was available at that time. The people believed if they built a tower high enough that they would see the face of God. In other words, man through his own rational structures and technology could obtain utopian bliss. As the story goes God came down and confounded the language so no one knew what the other was saying. Was it that each man spoke a different language or was it that conversation and language while remaining the same become so complexly differentiated and specialized that empathetic understanding was impossible? Whether this story is religiously prophetic or a sociological commentary the point still remains. When a society abandons subjective dynamic language systems for an objectified static language system, aimed at some rational utopian goal of social Darwinism, then the ability to communicate is lost, except only in a superficial manner. Feelings, morals, and empathy are diminished from language systems; thus symbols only are elevated to a high position and reality is ignored. The flow of information cannot be reciprocal, but exists as a power directive from the structures top to its bottom negating the social being. Regardless of how many like incidences of this phenomenon have occurred throughout history, man's will to control others has kept him making this fundamental error. It is almost as if egotistical godhood besieges every generation. Consequently the problem is not the ability to speak and use language, but to really understand what is being said and understanding the context of the statement. The more bureaucracy seeks to homogenize language the less the language is understood.

Bureaucratization refers to changes in the various organizations of society toward rationality. This ideally means improving efficiency and more effective attainment of common goals (Etizen, 1974). The term "common goals" is questionable, when the flow of information and ideas is only in one direction--top to bottom. The so-called common goals have been engineered, as well as the fulfillment of those goals. Such a power structure is asocial with respect to reciprocal social interaction. The dynamics of reciprocity between internal loci of meaning and external loci of structural constraints is thrown out of balance so that all meaning which is considered to be valid is externally imposed.

Etizen (1974) believes that participation is based on fear, not loyalty. This is not surprising with the bureaucratic structure. Loyalty develops through dynamic social interaction, while fear is derived through static relationships based on the power stratum, the dominant to the submissive, and the chain of legitimized commands. Through a process of bureaucratization the major social institutions that once maintained some plurality for the separation of power, as a check and balance system, have had their ideologies homogenized. By structuring society in a legal-rational framework, emphasis is diverted from personal meaning (content) and shifted to policy adherence, record keeping, and the appearance of order (form).

The loneliness that individuals feel in society is brought about then by the formalness of social relations. The strict adherence to rules, impersonal justice, and segmented relations ignores and disallows meaningful relations, the expression of emotions, caring of and being cared for by others (reciprocity).

The family group, though stark in its resistance to formal rational constraints, finds itself presently in danger. One need only look at divorce rates, child and spouse abuse, and marital discord. Bureaucracy has the effect of increasing its influence on the family to the point of diminished cooperation replaced by competition between children and spouses, overly authoritative handling of children, and rigid role structures. The consideration of persons as whole entities, dynamic in nature, has been replaced with myopic role definitions based on externally imputed "shoulds" and "should nots." This is not to denude role construction socially created and maintained. However, many roles are not created through an exchange but through a passive conformity to rational constructs and "mass media" mentality. Since individuals are alone, in terms of not being a "whole" person but a role in a viable group, they are much more susceptible to manipulation of the mass society. Examples of such control are numerous. Particularly good is The Selling of the President (McGinnis, 1968).

Hierarchies declare that as workers, most men and women must accept absolute authority and superiority of someone "above" them. The boss is not only empowered to tell a worker how to perform the work; the boss is also treated as a higher form of human being.

Comments are made of the "childishness" of the average adult in America. Bureaucracy not only convinces persons of their dependence, but demands dependence and childishness by the wholesale turning over of responsibility and self-respect to someone in authority (Reich, 1970).

The mechanism of bureaucratization for the achievement of social organization through efficiency on a massive scale cannot be deemed totally evil. Bureaucracy is efficient at handling many routine and predictable problems. The questions of legal-rational structures is not one of all or nothing. It is a question of the balance of that structure which will allow for individual dynamics and input. If the patterns of social behavior have been altered to the point that behavior is externally engineered for systems maintenance only, here is a short coming. The polarization of any form of control (external) to the extent that all other so called "contrary" forms are diminished or extinguished results in the loss of a person as a dynamically social being. Meaningless, powerlessness, felt isolation, and loneliness will continue to remain persistently a problem on a massive scale.

Secularization

Among various types of social change there is the change that took place within the religious institutions. It is important to examine the move from sacred orientations to secular orientations (Becker, 1932), as we investigate loneliness, for the religious institutions are so often thought of as important to the meaning and subjective experience of people.

During the middle ages, roughly from 1200 A.D. until 1450 A.D., society, which had been typically structured around the Roman Catholic Church, rebelled against central domination. According to Brinton (1960) secularization began to occur during the period.

> The late fifteenth, the sixteenth, and the seventeenth centuries are viewed as essentially transitional, essentially years in preparation for the Enlightenment. In this transition, humanism, Protestantism, and rationalism (the natural sciences) do their work of undermining the medieval, and preparing for modern cosmology (p. 27).

Increasing numbers of people were engaged in commerce. Such commerce was developed by networks globally, giving rise to inflated profits and easy wealth. Knowledge in all areas began to be assembled, classified, and made available. Philosophy began to view man as competitive by nature for honor and profit (Spann, 1950).

In the latter part of the seventeenth century, under pressure from new commercial and intellectual interests, religion was moving out of the foreground as a primary explanatory technique and being rapidly replaced with other scientific explanations. Concurrently, churches were moving from papal dominance to an increased subjection to the state, producing secular trends among the clergy. This appears to be the point that religion and secular thought became one, not as a synthesis but by the dilution of religious trends into state and intellectual conformity.

The eighteenth century brought about the settlement of North America. However, there was such a surge of the new development on the American "Frontier" that religion suffered. America was seeking to control the resources of nature, increase industrial power, and further provide new technology. Along with these developments came the growth of commerce, the rapid expansion of poorly governed cities, and the acquisition of enormous wealth by a few. In response to business and monetary monopoly by a small group, Christianity made two major changes. First, there was increased efficiency of organization in the churches under the influence of business methods and of lay activity in educational and benevolent enterprises. Second, it was an era of social gospelers who assailed the methods of the plutocrats and implored in the name of religion, change for economic justice and rights of the laborer (Sweet, 1948). Conversely, we see that the religious institutions were working for the rights of citizens but at the same time they were becoming the same, structurally, as the government they sought to confront. As society progressed away from a joint effort of church and state, it took on certain characteristics from the resultant secularity. None of the basic concerns of man's spirit (subjective reality) carried more than an attenuated relationship to religion. A unified religious spirit had lost its intensity. The objective habits of science, the routine character of industry, and the mechanistic influence of the machine had all increasingly encouraged the secularization of the West. Work was no longer surrounded by ritualism with religious connotations. The dance, song, and community spirit of work had been delated, leaving only drudgery in sight.

Secularization, according to Martin (1978), had a corrosive impact on visible religion consisting of two phases:

The first phase left all kinds of human scale structures standing: the family firm, self-employment, the small farm, the small office, the intimate college, and pockets of community, either rural organized around the church or industrial organized around the kinship network. All these were congruent with a family model of society where individuals mattered in religion to a constraining structure which could offer meaning (p. 91).

With the first phase came voluntary associations, life organizations, life organized by national boundaries, and a continuance of homogeneous feelings of brotherhood. The second phase of secularization had at its basis a breakdown of traditional authority with movement into legal-rational structures (Weber, 1922). As a result of this second phase, the human scale structures were broken down and replaced by bureaucracies; empathy through mass communication became apathy, and the national identity corroded (Martin, 1978).

This phase of secularization has three overall aspects that tend to be exhibited by society. They are the lack of unity (decreased emphasis on generalism and a move toward specialization), no superstition (the negation of unseen subjectivity), and alienation (meaning and definition loss) (Miller, 1963).

The lack of unity resulted in the consciousness of man undergoing a radical differentiation by which the various component parts of his psyche "broke loose" and moved into an independent freedom. The aesthetic and political sense was no longer dominated by religious themes, and reason developed science and repudiated any authority but truth considered "objectively." Each stood in diametric opposition to the religious unity that had traditionally held them in bounds, with the exception of one characteristic: the legal-rational structuring for control. Religion, while stressing its opposition to other social institutions, began to be studied and constructed in a polarized, objective position.

The lack of superstition and mystery is increasingly being eradicated by the further imposition by science and technology. We have learned a degree of honesty, how to observe objectively, and how to describe more accurately. This acts as a check on fears, exaggerations, and projections. However, there is a negative repercussion from a swing too far in this direction: we accept epistemological constructs that are dependable and repetitive, and reject everything that cannot be measured, analyzed, and predicted. Science and the polarization in the rational pushes away the unmeasurable as unknowable, and the sacred-religious is affected by reductions in worship as being trite. The negation of metaphysics is a dimension of secularization.

How have counter-religious ideologies been propagated so as to remove the importance of religion into an objectified polarity? The decrease in mystery with advances in technology undoubtedly played a role in the negation of metaphysical epistemological structures. Where a society dichotomizes content from form, retaining only form, we then find technique to be more important than basic understanding. In every area the symptom of a loss of content is indicated by the rise of technique. Techniques for control, manipulation, short cuts, speed and efficiency, and mass propaganda are ever increasing. Technique is a method employed to reduce the content of any reality being dealt with in order to handle it quickly. Civilizations that seek the control and efficiency of the society develop similarly until the actions of the people are increasingly channeled into routine and habit. In science this developed into technical research with its ever increasing use of symbols taken to be reality. However, description and labels given to various parts of the natural world are not explanation. In institutional religion it is exhibited by ecclesiastical secularity which is paramount in "letter of the law religion" for the control of participants but lacks the "spirit of the law" (Miller, 1963).

The objectification of religion for the control of individuals has its foundations in the Judeo-Christian tradition. Hierarchies and competition with nature are pervasive in Christian doctrine and the perception of diety. Consider the following example which contrasts the Tao of oriental philosophy with the almighty God of Christian religion:

> The great Tao flows everywhere to the left and to the right. All things depend upon it to exist, and it does not abandon them. To its accomplishments it lays no claim. It loves and nourishes all things, but does not lord over them.

On the other hand:

> His eyes were as a flame of fire, and on his head were many crowns; and he had a name written, that no man knew, but himself. And he was clothed with a vesture dipped in blood;

and his name is called the Word of God . . . And out of his mouth goeth a sharp sword, that with it he should smite the nations: and he shall rule them with a rod of iron; and he treadeth the winepress of the fierceness and wrath of Almighty God. And he hath on his vesture and on his thigh a name written: KING of KINGS, AND LORD of lords.

Magnificient as this is, the style is utterly different from the Taoist conception of the monarch, who is to:

Blunt his sharpness:
Get rid of his separateness;
Soften his brillance;
Be even with the dust.
This is called the profound identity

For,
The ruler who wants to be above the people must speak of himself as below them. If he wants to be ahead of the people, he must keep behind them. Thus when the sage is above, the people do not feel him as a burden, when he is ahead, the people do not feel him as a hindrance (pp. 38-39).

Note the extremely different concepts of deity. The Tao seems to be based on cooperation, love, and nourishment. The Christian conception is one of "rods of iron," smitten nations, wrath, fire, and fierceness. These differences in religious orientation toward deity, it would seem, are reflected in power positions and the institutional arrangements of American society. The control through objectification has developed throughout the social institutions since the period of Enlightment.

In this process of social change a controversy exists between those who maintain that a power elite are the controlling force in the rational power structures or whether upon reaching the top of the structure we find nobody is in charge. If we maintain that society is controlled by an elite few, there is a vested interest in swaying society into control. Domhoff (1974) diagrammatically modeled the transferral of power from a minute few elite into secular areas, with rational systems as the mechanism (Figure 6). The control, being so subtle and pervasive, is hard to pinpoint. However, it represents a radical shift in the way persons are treated, citizens to employer, the state, and institutions, particularly the rational control structures under the guise of religion and education. It is a shift from direct to indirect methods of control, from moralistic to mechanistic, from hortatory to manipulative (Schrag, 1978). Where society moves out of realism into a world of symbols and nominalism, taken to be real, the shift has been made by the controlling ideology. The resultant lack of satisfaction, meaning, and identity in the use of abstractions as adequate reflections of reality account for the glut of imagery for control. When real currency is scarce, counterfeit will increase without limit. Society, increasingly is deprived of profound, authentic and truly sacred images, which are

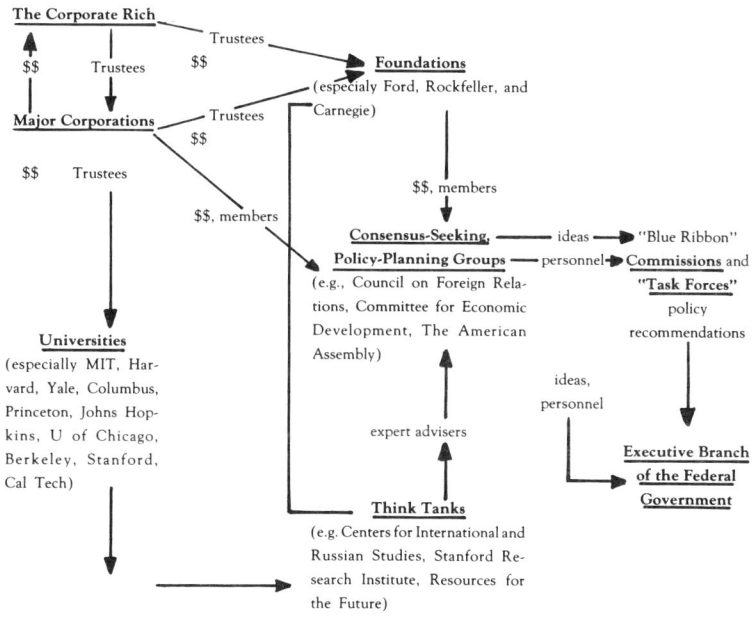

Figure 6. The Power Elite Policy-Making Process

socially, not institutionally, derived. Yet counterfeit images are abundant (Miller, 1963):

> Magazines are now full of pictures instead of words; television has taken the place of radio; the church world, public relations, social relations and politics are full of audio-visual aids and manipulated insinuations of popular images . . . All that once was poetry has now been demeaned, in selling sausage, hair spray and male deodorant, with market place control for power the ultimate goal (p. 72.

Whether we maintain that there is elite control or that legal-rational systems have nobody specifically directing them, the difficulties of overrationalization and the subsequent denial of man as a dualistic dynamic individual still remain.

The impact of secularization is brought into perspective if we look at the secular alterations of Christian doctrine. Ideally, Christian doctrine expresses the belief in new testament scripture. According to this idea, Christ himself brought a new mode of behavior and example which superseded the old testament teachings. Examples such as "do unto others as you would have them do unto you" are at the basis of Christianity. Notice the reciprocal, social nature of such a statement. Under the guise of religion today we find a shift has occurred, expressed by the most prominent leaders of religious institutions. Ideas of "more punishment of crime" or "more law and order" are frequently espoused from the pulpit. These ideas have not come from new testament doctrine but from old testament doctrine of "an eye for an eye and a tooth for a tooth." If Christian religion is indeed new testament oriented, why is the rhetoric of an old testament brand? Religious institutions clammer about "justice" as the old testament teachings, but little is said of "mercy" as contained in new testament doctrine. The author previously referred to this as "the letter of the law" (justice, rational rule) and the "spirit of the law" (mercy, subjective feelings). Christian religion emphasizes both as a dynamic; secularized, institutionalized religion emphasizes only the polarized, static concept of "justice." Religion thus has been incredibly altered away from the social by institutionalization and mechanisms of bureaucracy.

The thought processes in thinking have polarized in the dialectic extremes. Secularization of religion is not excluded from this polarization. Social change as characterized by rational constructs heretofore have disallowed a dynamic form of thinking to continue. According to Chapman (1971):

> When a person views the world as a dynamic process to be examined from its general aspects to its particular aspects and from the particular to the general by way of a conceptual method of thought, he will see it quite differently than when he uses the dialectical method of thought where his ability to think is severely eroded. This erosion of individual ability to think from the general to the particular and from the particular to the general is a result in the dialectical method of thought. The dialectic has a built-in tendency to shunt thought into a polar position where thought and emotion rise to guard a vested interest position (pp. 71-72).

Man now finds himself in a polarized existence of rational constructs. Conceptual thinking, as opposed to dialectical thought allows for the dynamic relationship between the poles of reality construction, meaning, and identity. The polar position of rational constructs exists for modern man as the irrational aspects of daily experience are lost. This is not due to the nature of reality only being "rational", but the weakness in allowing only the rational to be valid appraisal of reality to the exclusion of anything else.

Social Change and the Polarized Dialectic

Let us consider the dialectic of man's existence. We say that dialectic is a method of considering reality. The essence of the dialectic is contradiction; each concept implies its opposite (Turner and Beeghley, 1981). Usually, dialectic models consist of ideas as antonyms, that is, opposites. Dialectical methods usually, consists of a thesis, an antithesis, and a systhesis. The actual splitting of a concept cannot be done except for the sake of objective analysis. Though, as discussed previously, dialectical methods as opposed to conceptual methods usually result in a polarized reality construction. The polarization occurs as bipolar constructs are collapsed or synthesized into a single pole construct (Chapman, 1971).

As we try to develop a theoretical model for loneliness, it will be necessary to present polar concepts as a mode of comparison which reflect the situated rational constructs that dominate modern trends.

Figure 7 contains several polar concepts of man. Is man rational or irrational, compulsive or impulsive, objective or subjective, structured or unstructured, controlled by an external locus or internal locus? Several constructs can be included in the polar extremes which

The general	or	The particular
The empirical	or	The abstract
The map	or	The territory
The symbol	or	The referent
The thought	or	The thing
The construct	or	Reality
The concept	or	The world
Community	or	Society
Ideal	or	Real
True	or	False
Good	or	Evil
Time	or	Space
God	or	Devil
Life	or	Death
Light	or	Darkness
One	or	Many
Perception	or	Hallucination
Form	or	Content
Functional	or	Dysfunctional
The medium	or	The message
Structure	or	Function
Conscious	or	Unconscious
Rational	or	Irrational
Subjective	or	Objective
Intrinsic	or	Extrinsic
Epistemology	or	Ontology
Heredity	or	Environment
Nature	or	Nurture

Figure 7. Dialectical Conflicts

constitute a duality of existence or reality. Horton (1966) has used a similar method in discussing the differences between assumptions underlying functionalism and conflict theories of sociology.

Were we to polarize a human being's existence to either extreme, would we not negate many aspects of reality as nonexistent or inconsequential? Man's existence is not an either-or situation but a "both" existence. Man is a dynamic individual. The need for expression, meaning, and social interaction relies on the combination of both antithetical extremes. The meaning so often sought lies in the dynamic interchange or interdependency of the mental constructs. Consider Figure 8 below. If a shift is made too far toward either static construct, duality or reality has been hampered or negated. Man's nature includes all of the constructs from both static positions and more. No listing of nominal symbols can fully characterize the total existence of man.

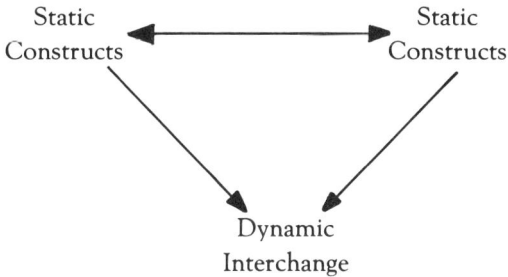

Figure 8. Dual Mental Constructs

Legal-rational systems, that characterize the major social institutions, are anything but dynamically social. Polarization has ocurred, negating not only the other construct extreme but the dynamic position requires that each construct extreme be tempered by the other. Without the tempering that provides a balance, society in terms of a social dynamic and heterogeneous exchange has been homogenized. Feelings of "who am I" arise. The complexity of social reality has been reduced to a simplistic construct. What better way is there to control meanings, ideas, beliefs, than by defining the total of social reality as a static construct, and by stigmatization of those who do not fit into the construct.

Where man's existence is viewed as either rational or irrational, we find a dialectical conflict with no synthesis possible. Figure 7 illustrates the tendency to dichotomize and then to embrace one side of the dichotomy to the exclusion of the other or to choose one position in a range of possibilities, rejecting the whole range as irrelevant or nonexistent. Such is the case with scientific rational structures which choose a point of reality on an infinite range and call it "absolute truth" or "social facts."

The dialectical synthesis is possible only when man's nature is viewed as rational and irrational. Thus, the synthesis will take into account the social dynamic (Figure 8). Power to control a large number of people may be usurped by eliminating alternative sources of social attachments and beliefs, particularly the subjective aspects (Wrong, 1970). The irrationality of a rational system that seeks to maintain a rigid chain of static order is described in the following (Kolakowski, 1977):

> Its integration was idential with its disintegration; it was perfectly integrated in that all forms of collective life were subordinated to, and imposed by, one ruling center; and it was perfectly disintegrated from the same reason: civil society was virtually destroyed, and the citizens, in all their relations with the state, faced an omnipotent apparatus as isolated and powerless individuals (p. 285).

The above description of Stalinism is seen as a totalitarian state. By the use of the techniques of persuasion and the mechanisms of communications, the social person is bereft of social attachments and many times unknowingly manipulated by the persons who control power. Whether we speak of Communism, Capitalism, Stalinism, or any other "ism," where an "omnipotent apparatus" has been elevated to total control, the individuals within these systems become "isolated and powerless." Jackson (1976) notes:

> One of the principle means used by capitalistic societies to maintain their exploitation and oppression of people has been to secure the cooperation of different groups of people in oppressing each other. This has been done by instilling and maintaining attitudes of racism, prejudice, sexism, and adultism between the different sections of the oppressed population. Under capitalism the oppressed have to oppose

each other. The oppressors are not numerous enough; they must deceive the people they victimize into doing it to each other (p. 46).

The move to a polarized national thought process which is then manipulated by those in power for the control of resources has affected, through social change, the ability of the individual to maintain a balanced reality between polarized constructs. Identity and meaning have been hidden from view for the purpose of control. Loneliness is a symptom of the forced polarization of man against himself.

Summary

This chapter has attempted to show through various aspects of social change how the duality of man's existence has progressively become imbalanced and polarized into the rational. Loneliness, if it is a feeling of loss, isolation, alienation, and meaninglessness, has a subjective base. If the subjective side of the individual has been progressively negated, then a typology of the various types of loneliness can be generally described by the focus upon the aspects of that negation.

In Chapter IV, emphasis will be placed on three general types of loneliness: (1) situationally imposed loneliness, (2) other imposed loneliness, and (3) self-imposed loneliness or aloneness. The condition (external) and the characteristics of the affected individual (internal) will be presented. These typologies will not be totally discrete, as they vary in magnitude and intensity with each person.

CHAPTER IV

A THEORETICAL TYPOLOGY AND DESCRIPTION OF LONELINESS

In this chapter three general types of loneliness will be examined: (1) situational or structual imposed loneliness, (2) other imposed loneliness, and (3) self-imposed loneliness or aloneness.

In order to present the typologies and a subsequent model in a meaningful scheme, each typology will be discussed individually.

The Bipolar Nature of Man

This author has sought to demonstrate the bipolarity of man. The alteration that has occured through social change and institutional structures have and are presently negating this dynamic social nature. Such a negation is at the base of loneliness. The self is reduced from an "I"-"Me" balance to only a receiving "me" (Chapman, 1972). The directives of "other" are the only constructs which, given enough power to impose, are considered to be valid.

It was Sorokin (1966), who maintained that sociocultural phenomena includes the three component types of personality, society, and culture. These components are mutually interdependent and dynamic. Many sociologists, most notably Parsons (1951) have taken these processes and by use of a rational scheme have placed them into a "cybernetic hierarchy." When one of these component parts is placed artifically into a rational hierarchy, the other components are dependent on the one part for their reification. The mutual dynamic is thus replaced with a static directive. Indications of such a departure are . . .

". . . where meaningful interaction between two or more individuals is reduced to a one-way directive between a person and a machine or a person and mass media, particularly T.V. or a person and a technique such as a bureaucratic hierarchy in which the machine, mass media, or technique is always dominant. Other departures are indicated when among the component parts of personality, society, and culture, culture is artifically elevated to the top of a fixed hierarchy or order in which society and personality are always subordinate.

Again departure is indicated where one part, as for example the person, is split into component parts of rational and irrational with one part of the dichotomy elevated to perpetual dominance, or where one part of the dichotomy is dropped out of the scheme entirely, and the remaining part is magnified to be the whole. Other departures are indicated where a man's total needs are rationally pre-arranged in a fixed hierarchy, for example, his economic needs are always dominant over religious needs, and so on, or where culture is split into the component parts of ideational and material with material culture always leading ideational culture or the other way around." (Chapman, 1971, pp. 2-3).

Loneliness, alienation, and meaninglessness are the results of one part of man's bipolar, dichotomous nature being elevated to perpetual dominance. In this case the logical-empirical domination has been elevated to the negation of any other social action, thought, or mental construct.

Situationally-imposed and other-imposed types of loneliness are particularly present as a polarized construct of logic, empiricism, overrationalization, and structures are imposed on the individual. Self-imposed loneliness then becomes a reaction to the polarized rationalism with a shift to the other extreme of irrationalism, structurelessness, nonconformity, and subjectivism, in combination with each other or individually.

Within the framework of Figure 9, situationally-imposed loneliness and other-imposed loneliness have been aligned at the same pole of the dichotomy, while self-imposed loneliness is arranged at the other pole. The question that might be raised is, "why are situationally-imposed loneliness and other-imposed loneliness dichotomized into the same area or extreme?"

Ideally, norms, values, and beliefs are consensually derived through interaction with other social beings (Horton, 1966). Figure 9 illustrates the dynamic between the self, other, and the situation or structure. Observe that others constitute the dynamic center of a dichotomy between self and structure. Polarization to either extreme results in a static interaction, negating the dynamic reciprocity. As demonstrated in the discussion of social change, the shift has been toward the situation-structural pole for the "rational" control and then prediction of society. The self is thus negated. The alignment of other-imposed loneliness and situationally-structurally-imposed loneliness becomes the present-day model. The position of other-imposed social action has moved toward the situationally-structurally-imposed social action.

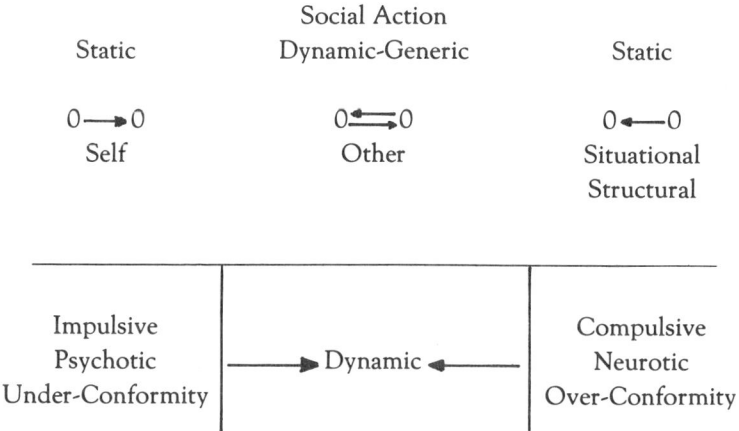

Figure 9. Ideal-Typic Dynamic of Social Action

Others who impose social action and subsequently loneliness do so not out of consensual society reciprocity, as in the ideal typic model (Figure 9), but because they themselves have imposed the situational constraints imposed on them (Figure 10). Thus, norms, values, and beliefs become disconsensual. What is right, good, or true for others is based on the situational-structural power directive. What becomes normative are those actions and beliefs that are directed by the persons in control of the structure. Castigation, negative sanctions, and coercion are applied to those who would suggest and act in an alternative manner to the structural power directive. Consider the following example. The family, of all groups, should be socially reciprocal. There are few persons who would disagree with such a statement, though in many instances the effects of the structural

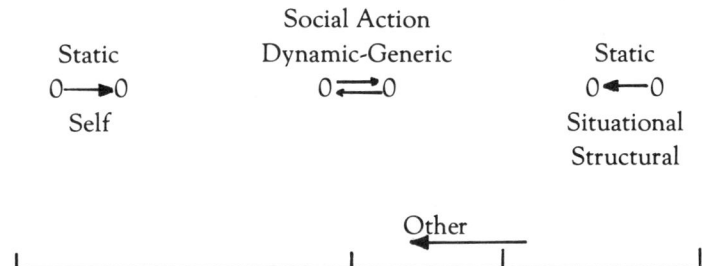

Figure 10. Present-Day Polarization of Social Action

imposition are destroying these bonds. After working in a bureaucratic chain of imputed commands during the day, a parent returns home only to continue the imposition of directives on the family (Figure 11).

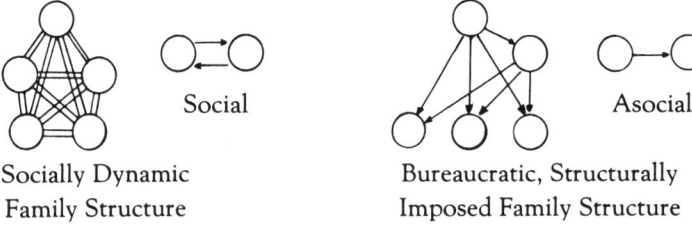

Figure 11. Social and Asocial Familial Structures

The bureaucratic mentality of power directives is projected into the family structure from the work place. External pressures outside the family thus influence its breakdown by introduction of asocial structuring. Primary social relations, the social bond of interdependence, consequently has been progressively negated. The major social institutions which were once created to insure survival for the basic family organization as secondary tools have become primary, leaving the family as secondary. Loneliness, as with other major social problems, is a consequential symptom of this structural shift in emphasis and hierarchial construction.

Let us examine the typologies of structurally-situationally-imposed loneliness, other-imposed loneliness, and self-imposed loneliness. For the sake of clarity each type will be described in relation to the social institutions of the family, school, religion, government, and industry. The types are not meant as totally discrete variables, but as general frames of references for the understanding of loneliness.

Structurally-Situationally-Imposed Loneliness

The descriptive character of the person exhibiting loneliness with its roots in the structure and situation can best be understood by examining the character of modern industrial man and the demands placed on him. Several authors have described the modern, industrial man as a "marketing character" (Fromm, 1976), the "organization man" (Whyte, 1956), and the "corporate man" (Reich, 1970). Though the nomenclature varies there is a striking similarity in the character traits of such persons.

Fromm (1976) terms modern man as a marketing character because this type of person experiences himself as a commodity, and one's value is not "use value" but "exchange value." Man has become a commodity on the "personality market." Success depends largely on how well persons sell themselves on the market; how well they get their "personality" across; how nice a "package" they are; whether they are "cheerful," "sound," "aggressive," "reliable," "ambitious;" furthermore, what their family backgrounds are, what clubs they belong to, and whether they know the "right people." The loss of self is insured by the structural constraints of the market. Fromm (1976) explains:

> What shapes one's attitude toward oneself is the fact that skill and equipment for performing a given task are not sufficient; one must be able to win in competition with many others in order to have success. If it were enough for the purpose of making a living to rely on what one knows and what one can do, one's self-esteem would be in proportion to one's capacities, that is, to one's use value.

But since success depends largely on how one sell's one's personality, one experiences oneself as a commodity or, rather, simultaneously as the seller and the commodity to be sold. A person (in such a structure) is not concerned with his or her life and happiness, but with becoming salable (p. 133).

The aim of the marketing character is to completely adapt or become infinitely malleable so as to be desirable under all conditions of the personality market (I believe most clinicians would call this neurosis). This is very much life Goffman's dramaturgical model of "life as a con-game" (Goffman, 1959). However, does the individual decide to be a market personality or does the structure impose overconformity and rationalization on the individual as a prerequisite for success?

Those under the imposition of the rational structure where success is defined as economic security are without goals except moving and doing things with the greatest rational efficiency. If asked why they must move so fast, why things have to be done with the greatest efficiency, they have no genuine answer but offer rationalizations, such as "to create more jobs" or "to keep the company growing" (Fromm, 1976). The identity and self of such individuals "is" the organization. The bipolarity of the self is negated. Rational economic structures become the point of primary validity. Little interest is shown in philosophical or religious questions, such as "where have we come from," "why amd I living," or "why am I going this direction rather than another." Yet though such questions are rarely asked, the inner-self, bipolar in nature, responds to the forced polarization of the self by the structure with symptoms of stress, nervous breakdowns, heart ailments, or ulcers. Other responses to the structural impositions are escapism in fantasy, television, or perhaps more deleteriously, drugs and alcohol. Characteristically:

> . . . "They have their big, ever-changing egos, but none has a self, a core, a sense of identity. The "identity crisis" of modern society is actually the crisis produced by the fact that its members have become selfless instruments, whose identity rests upon their participation in the corporations(or other giant bureaucracies). Where there is no authentic self, there can be no identity." (Fromm, 1976, p. 134)

As the constraints of the rational structuring of society increase, the need for outlets of escape will also probably increase. For persons to retain a balanced self, a compensation must be made for the impositions of the legal-rational structures. Emotionalism, irrational thought, creativity, and fantasy, by whatever means will be a necessary outlet for the balancing of the self.

It is in this respect that increased rational constraints increases in social control legislation, and law enforcement will prove ineffective. The more laws and rational structure a society imposes on its people the more they will disregard law as insignificant and will increasingly act out in a lawless and irrational manner. They must, as a balancing act in their own minds. Too many laws means lawlessness; a point that points in too many directions is the same as no point at all.

The "irrational" emotions which are old fashioned do not well fit into the scheme of selling and exchanging or have no function according to the logic of the machine of which they are part. The question for the structure to impose is "how well do you function," bestowing advancement in the bureaucracy on those who function best by structural definitions. The self under such circumstances can only become alienated, existentially wanton, and lonely. Albert Schweitzer explains:

> Because society with its developed organization exercises a hitherto unknown power over man, man's dependency on it has grown to a degree that he almost has ceased to live a mental (geistig) experience on his own. . . Thus we have entered a new Middle Ages. By a general act of will freedom of thought has been put out of function, because many give up thinking as free individuals, and are guided by the collective to which they belong. . . With the sacrifice of independence of thought we have - how could we be otherwise - lost faith in truth. Our intellectual - emotional life is disorganized. The overorganization of our public affairs culminates in the organization of thoughtlessness. (Schweitzer, 1923, p. 24)

So irrational is the total rationalization of existence by structural imposition that characteristics of alienation, identity problems, and loneliness may become and are a rational response. The paradox of such responses is that modern man sets out as an endless search, it would seem, for identity and awareness of self-thinking, all the while believing that such is to be found through more conformity, more competition, more economic gain, and by subjugation to the structural impositions of a rational power scheme. By analogy, the closer modern man perceives the butterfly or self identity to be, the farther it has flown away, for the butterfly dangles on a structural string of greed and power for profit and control.

Could modern man be such a masochist for a structural sadism? Masochistic strivings appear as inferiority, powerlessness, and individual insignificance. The compulsive, neurotic, overcomformer is basically of a masochistic type (Reich, 1933; Horney, 1956; Horkheimer, 1936). The sadism within the structure is a characteristic of the same masochist at varying times. Three aspects of sadism are: (1) to make others dependent on oneself and to have absolute and unrestricted power over them; (2) the impulse not only to rule over others in an absolute fashion, but to exploit them, use them, steal from them, to "disembowerl" them, and (3) to make others suffer or to see them suffer (Fromm, 1941). The sadist needs the person over whom he rules, since his own feeling of strength is rooted in the fact that he is master over someone. Both masochistic and sadistic feelings tend to help the individual to escape his unbearable feelings of loneliness, aloneness, and powerlessness. The cycle is vicious, for by increasing masochism and sadism, the individual, while "feeling temporarily secure," has moved farther from self-identity, which in turn will give use to new strivings for masochism and sadism, for security, and so on. Thus, in a rational power structure the superior in the work place, for example, gives a command (sadism) to a subordinae (masochism) who in turn gives a command (saidsm) to his subordinate (masochism). The whistle blows to end the day; each participant in the structure returns home and demands (sadism) that the spouse and children subordinate (masochism) to them. Furthermore, the children must find a subordinate for the chain of sado-masochism to continue; consequently, they "kick the dog." This is particulary descriptive of the means by which a bureaucratic power structure is continually infesting the primary survival group, the family, to its demise. The sado-masochism inherent in a power structure, which maintains a chain of command, forces the surrender of one's own self and renounces all strength and pride connected with the self. In such total dependency, one loses one's integrity as an individual and surrenders freedom; but one gains a new security and a new pride in the participation in the power in which they are submerged. The benefit is "security" against the torture of doubt (Fromm, 1941). Yet in this position the loss of identity, pride, and moral responsibility are consequential. The moral responsibility is to the maintenance of the organization.

The rationalization of the individual whose self has been negated by the structure lies in attributing human characteristics to the structure. According to Whyte (1956), the pressures of society have been morally legitimated against the individual because of three propositions accepted in modern thought: a belief in the group as a source of creativity, a human's ultimate need to "belong," and the application of science to achieve human belongingness.

Creativity and belongingness may, in fact, be essential for man; but the belief that scientifically rationalized structures can be a greater sum than its constituent parts, the individual's, negates the uniqueness and identity of each person. To manipulate persons scientifically in order to achieve creativity and belongingness is a contradiction in terms. Unlike the rational structuring of science, creativity and belongingness are socially derived through rational and irrational means.

In The Greening of America, Reich (1970) presents us with a picture of man's development through consciousness levels. The "corporate man" is desribed as believing:

> that the present American crisis can be solved by greater commitment of individuals to the public interest, more social responsibility by private business, and, above all, by more affirmative government action--regulation, planning, more of a welfare state, better and more rational administration and bureaucracy. . . Behind a facade of optimism there is a profoundly pessimistic view of man (p. 70)

The "pessimism" is revealed by the continued Hobbesian notion that since man is aggressive, power seeking, and competitive, that he must be controlled. However, the very structures that strive in this endeavor are the genesis of much of the existing aggression and power seeking. Insistence is made that what man produces by means of reason--the state, laws, technology, manufactured goods--constitutes the true reality. What is good, moral, and justice are those polarized concepts of reason, the rational, the empirical, the structured, and the bureaucratic.

The central ideology of these structurally-situationally-imposed directives is one of technology, the domination of man and environment by technique. Science, technology, organization, and planning are of prime importance. The question is not one of cooperation but of control by structural technique. Nor is it a question of mutual interdependence, which allows the self to develop, but exploitation for power and material acquisition by the systematic imposition of power directives. Though the structure is, ideally, rational and logical, human existence cannot be supported on the basis of any single principle such as this demands (Reich, 1970).

This one-dimensionality (Marcuse, 1964) that the rational structure demands, imposes an existence of "security," "logic," and "belongingness." Though many persons involved with these structures speak of group efforts and goals, the mind is not fooled. The symptoms of man as "structural material" are alienation and loneliness. But when questioned about such ailments, particularly loneliness, the individual denies fear, separation from self, and isolation within a group of people. People believe their identity to be within the conforming behavior to the single-minded corporate state (Reich, 1970). Surely physical ailments would indicate that the demands of the structural corporate state are negating the basic identity needs of the individual. It seems to be in the quiet hours of self-reflection that such persons ask, "What is happening to me?" or "What am I doing?" More often the conclusion is that the person cannot cope. Perhaps, the conclusion should be that the structural impositions have forced one to negate oneself for the control of one's faculties. This may explain the executive who materially has everything and suddenly realizes he has nothing. Such a dilemma is illustrated by Robinson (1956) in a poem entitled "Richard Cory":

> Whenever Richard Cory went to town
> We people on the pavement looked at him:
> He was a gentleman from sole to crown,
> Clean favored, and imperially slim.
>
> And he was always quietly arrayed.
> And he was always human when he talked;
> But still he fluttered pulses when he said,
> 'Good Morning,' and he glittered when he talked.
>
> And he was rich -- yes, richer than a king--
> And admirably schooled in every grace:

> In fine, we thought that he was everything
> To make us wish that we were in his place.
>
> So on we worked, and waited for the light,
> And went without the meat, and cursed the bread;
> And Richard Cory, one calm summer night
> Went home and put a bullet through his head (p. 19).

The discrepancy that occurs between the life we desire and the life we actually experience brings anxiety and loneliness to our existence. It seems that we always want something that we do not have. But this lack of contentment with one's existence is a demand imposed upon us. The structure of capitalism must instill these desires constantly for the continuity of control and ideological self-perpetuation. This is basic to the "marketing character," the Corporate Man, the lonely alienated person who supposes that self-definition and acceptance is always just ahead as long as he remains rationally tied to the structure-logic.

Consider the factory worker who has developed a reciprocal friendship among his peers on the assembly line. He is chosen to be the new foreman over those he had worked alongside for several years. He has faithfully served the organization where he is employed. Through organizationally defined merit, he has been chosen to oversee those he played poker with on Friday nights, went bowling with on Monday nights, and with whom he interacted during his off-work hours. However, the organizational placement affects his informal life style. With more money he may move to another area of town, express contempt for those who were once close friends, and find that new "friends" are made only at the same level as his--that of foreman. He finds himself with less off-work friends, except those who occupy the same positions organizationally defined. What were once unbreakable bonds of comradeship are now loosened. The primary reciprocal interaction socially derived has thus been superseded by the secondary linear directive asocially constructed by the organization. This is not without severe costs, for the person has vested more of an identity into the power structure of the organization. Role demands are set which disallow for socially derived bonds of interaction. Loneliness is endemic to America, because the institutions and their organization demand the very homogeneous values, beliefs, and actions that insure the loss of self by redefining for the individual what in "reality" constitutes the "true self."

Structurally-Situationally-Imposed Loneliness and Social Institutions

The family is a social institution which by its very existence and processes insures the survival of the larger society. Members of the family group are bound by a loyalty to cooperate and assist each other and to place each other's interests above those of outsiders (Linton, 1936). Mutual interdependence, adjustment, deliberation, and resolve are tied together by bonds of affections and common interest. The structure of the family is not one in which the heads of a household are always dominant or rigid but flexible, accommodating themselves to the most timid thoughts, acts, and emotions of each member of the family, especially those members most helpless and needy (Chapman, 1972).

The structural-situational impositions on the family group force this accommodating reciprocity between family members to crystallize into rigid linear chains of power relations. As was described earlier (Figure 12), the influence of the structure external to the family has become increasingly imposing so as to break down the social dynamics of accommodation and sensitivity into inflexibility and rigidity between family members. Families thus begin to take on the characteristics of the organization. Mistrust replaces trust, competition replaces cooperation, insatiable want replaces contentment. The structural-situational impositions of the institutional organization have taken personality and congealed it into a resource for systems needs of money. Every action and thought not needed by the system is repressed anew in each newborn child (Chapman, 1972).

Under such conditions the social process has been transformed into a hierarchy of rational rules for legitimate power. To define legitimate as only being that which is rational within the organization destroys the social process not only between individuals in the family group, but within each of their minds. The development of the self into its totality is disallowed. Many of the tensions that arise between parents, parents and siblings, and among the siblings are coming into the family group from the external structures in terms of job pressure, mass media, and consumerism, economic pressures, and discrepancies between externally imposed "life" (actual) versus desired life. The family group nonetheless is still struggling to maintain its socially cohesive existence. However, over the past 75 years we have seen a change from extended families to nuclear families and presently many single-parent families.

The deprivation of self for man begins, to its fullest extent, as institutionalized training begins in the public school. The object of training is not only to teach one how to perform some specific function; it is to make one become that function; to see and judge himself and others in terms of functions; and to abandon any aspect of self, thinking, questioning, feeling, or loving that has no utility for production or consumption in the corporate state (Reich, 1970). The training for a job within the structure of rational bureaucracy is just as important as the training for the role of consumer within the structure. Both are equally important for the "loss of self."

While learning to become an economic citizen who produces and consumes, the young person is taught about making a pseudo-self. That is, a self which will minimize the punishment of the organization and maximize the rewards of the corporate structure. What is moral and ethical is the ability to economically manipulate others and the position one achieves in the structure hierarchy.

The emphasis on position achieved instead of "living as a process" constitutes the basic difference between indoctrination and education, respectively. Teaching and education exist to help students think for themselves. Instruction and indoctrination are aimed at compelling the student to accept someone else's ideas or version of the "facts." Whenever a bad mark can be given for disagreement, indoctrination occurs through behavior modification techniques. This author recalls a particular English class in which the students, myself included, were asked to read a poem by Robert Frost. Subsequently we were to write down our interpretation of the poem or "What does Robert Frost mean and what is he saying in this poem?" The class worked fursiously to interpret Frost. Upon turning in the essays we were informed that there was a "right way" and a "wrong way" to interpret the poem. The Right way was, of course, the way in which the instructor interpreted the poem. The essays not paralleling this position received a low mark. To this day this author wonders how that instructor knew any better what was on Frost's mind than any other person in the class whose interpretations held proportionately as much validity. The instructor's knowledge of Frost's mind was accurate, because the institution had granted him authority that made it so. This is only an example, but the number of like examples is endless within the institutional training of the young person to fulfill roles and join the ranks of the rational structures.

Constant emphasis on externally defined "success" in terms of status, material possessions, and acceptability by others are key elements in training the young person to value structurally imposed constructions of reality. Good and bad, right and wrong ways of behaving are defined by external policy commands (law, mass media, rules) in which there is no allowance for questioning or social bargaining. While it is important for persons to learn concepts of good and bad, the difference lies in the structure imposing one idea of "good" or "right" and disallowing the social, dynamic construction of reality to occur between persons which is at constant change and tension over time. Rational structures are resistant to change, statically maintaining their control. Human beings are forced to adapt to the institution for its needs, instead of the institution adapting constantly to human needs.

Thus, self-identity moves away from the generic social level of person-to-person, and becomes a relationship of man to merit, man to machine, man to ideology, and man to techniques of economy and external directives asocially imputed (Chapman, 1972). The idea of critical thought to students is alien. If asked to complete a summary of readings or to reiterate material assigned for reading, the task is carried out with relative ease. However, when asked to read an article and then critique the same or to write a five-page paper expressing their opinion on a given topic, one is quick to observe that this is a foreign idea. Most students have not actively expressed themselves but have passively absorbed and regurgitated information. They are victims of indoctrination, not education. Creativity has been stifled as well as those aspects of the self not suitable for systems needs. The self now dissected responds with feelings of alienation, loneliness, worthlessness, and fear. The paradox of this structural-situational imposition is that for most, efforts are made to carry out tasks more quickly with more efficiency, increasing their conformity and obedience to the demands placed on them. However, the circle becomes vicious, for the more their definition of self parallels the "imposed" self, the more they have negated the unique aspects of their generic "social" self.

The imposition of authority, indoctrination, and training is not the most terrible aspect of the institution; it is the result of such domination. Consequently, as Reich (1970) explains, there is:

an all-out assault upon the newly emerging adolescent self. The self needs, above all, privacy, liberty, and a degree of sovereignty to develop . . . The school is a brutal machine for destruction of the self, controlling it, heckling it, hassling it into a thousand busy tasks, a thousand noisy groups, never giving it a moment to establish a knowledge within (p. 150).

For social survival the institution of education has the universal social responsibility of socialization (Young and Mack, 1959). But socialization implies reciprocal exchange, growth of self, abilities to consider, think, and observe. What passes for education is not socialization at all but "structuralization": it disallows important aspects of self to emerge, particularly if such aspects promote reconsideration of existing institutional "givens," imply change, or constantly question. After all, the self and consequently persons at the generic social level are not so easily given in to follow nor are they easily controlled where all aspects of self-identity exist.

In Chapter III, we discussed secularization and social change. The structural-situational imposition of institutionalized religion may be doing more to create a loss of self than gain self-identity; furthermore, it may instill "church-ism" but not religion. Religion is spontaneous, perennial, and a universal attribute of man arising from man experiencing uncertainty, insecurity, incompletion, and concern about the unknown and unexplained aspects of life (Chapman, 1972). A religious belief is a personal relationship between the person and some form of deity or supreme being. Each person religiously intereacts with an unseen supreme being or force to help resolve doubts, fears, and events which are outside scientific logic.

However, religion has moved out of the traditional realm of social life into a structural bantling of economics, bureaucracy, and hierarchies of authority and control. "Churchism" is the result. Characteristic of "churchism" are congregations more interested in clothing styles, evening socials, attending to their religion not for the sake of religion but for the sake of the "appearance" of religion. To become a religious leader in American society does not require a traditional society consensus of religiosity, nor charisma. It entails the state's magic wand of legitimacy through four years of college, a license, and other secular requirements. Churches professing religion have taken on corporate structures, money-gathering schemes through television, radio, and publications. With the exception of a few small sects, most denominations parallel the structure of the corporate state. For many, religion is "churchism" wound up on one day of the week with all the pomp and form of an executive corporate meeting. Included are discussions of budget, agendas, fund raisers, and how to bring others into the structural fold. Could it be that a deeply religious person with a self-felt social interaction with a supreme being would feel alienated, lonely, and perceive fakery amidst the ranks of the church goer. If the institution of religion has been constructed so as to impose a meritocracy, a hierarchy, and has aligned itself with the ideology of industry and government which is originally sought to oppose (See Chapter 3, secularization), it can be nothing more than prostitution under the guise of religion. With this style of prostitution form supercedes content, symbols supercedes reality, "legitimate" authority supercedes social interaction, and institutionalization exposes the church to be the corporate bastard child as it really exists. Loss of self, worthlessness low self-esteem and particulary guilt are insured by a "legitimized" church executive. Anderson (1970) describes the alienating contradiction of "churchism" in the following lyric entitled "Wind Up":

> When I was young, they packed me off to school
> and taught me how not to play the game.
> I didn't mind if they groomed me for success
> or it they said that I was just a fool.
> So I left there in the morning, with their God
> tucked underneath my arm,
> their half-assed smiles and their book of rules.
>
> So I asked this God a question and by way of firm reply
> He said 'I'm not the kind you have to wind up on Sundays.'
>
> So to my old headmaster (and anyone who cares)
> before I'm through I'd like to say my prayers.
> I don't believe you: you got the whole damn thing all wrong.
> He's not the kind you have to wind up on Sundays.
>
> Well you can excommunicate me on my way to Sunday school,
> and have all the bishops harmonize these lines.

> How do you dare to tell me that I'm my Father's son,
> When that was just an accident of birth
> I'd rather look around me compose a better song
> because that's the honest measure of my worth.
> In your pomp and all your glory you're a poorer man than me,
> As you lick the books of death born out of fear.
>
> I don't believe you: you got the whole damn thing all wrong.
> He's not the kind you have to wind up on Sundays.
> (Jethro Tull Aqualung)

Thus, the move away from a generic social religion to an ideal typic rational "churchism" has rendered the survival function of religion impotent. "Churchism" as a magic show casts illusions for those who will lend an ear, play the game, and contribute to the plate for future productions. Such is the ideology of "churchism." Through this institution comes the reduction of protestantism, via Max Weber, to a scheme for making money (Gerth and Mills, 1958). The victory of power as the value of the ideal type of organization requiring dependency relationships is the stuff "churchism" through institutionalization is made of.

The false sense of security provided by rational structures do more to remove the truly religious away from security and identity by polarizing the generic duality of self. It is unfortunate that religion is not immuned to this kind of ideological dissection. Loneliness as imposed by structural-situational "churchism" is the consequence of rationalizing the aesthetic. When the vicar exclaims, "Have faith in God," maybe he is really saying, "Believe in me and my structure, and my version of the story." Such an imposition destroys the "wholeness" of man, leaving him as a sponge rendered of all its water, left to dry, and blown by the wind of insecurity, isolated in the midst of many, desperate in the midst of few.

The political institution has as its function the preservation of order (Young and Mack, 1959). The rational guarantees are constructed to insure that the other social institutions, namely, the family, the school, the church, and the economy are protected in the prerogative to provide the society with attributes that insure survival. The political state, socially endowed, serves as a system of checks and balances. However, when the social-political state moves away from a social construction into a legal-rational political state, it elevates itself above considerations of the social. The checks and balances socially derived at the generic level are replaced by hierarchical power relations. The welfare of society consequently is now no longer a concern. Power and the welfare of power by dominating, impersonal, rational rule has become the elevated ideology by which society subscribes (Chapman, 1972).

The move from social welfare to power welfare, in effect, places the other social institutions into a dependency relationship to the political state. As social survival institutions are not needed, they will be systematically destroyed. Subjugation to this elevated legal-rational structuring separates man from his self-identity by reification of the social self to the legal-rational self. Persons are thus given a number, a rank, and the status of systems material. Great care is taken to use such ranks and numbers to reward those individuals who best conform to structural demands. The better one prostitutes oneself to the structure in terms of systems material, the more likely one is to increase one's status within that system.

More recently, with the advances in technology and the advent of computers, the capabilities of control by surveillance has become a reality (Miller, 1971). Information on "character" is constantly being gathered and filed by state agencies concerning "cooperation with others," "ethical standards," appropriateness of dress," "language and conduct," "ability to react constructively to criticism, suggestions, advice," "emotional stability." Such "file" materials accumulate through the years as an indicator of how legal-rational one has or has not become (Reich, 1970). Problems of self-identity, alienation, fear, and loneliness result as such structural-situational impositions are forced upon the self of each person.

The "good character," as defined by the state, is tense, rigid, narrowly limited, specialized, and dependent in fear to the state. Competence, worth, esteem, and the ability to cope are set into goals which are past- or future-oriented. The orientation of the present or "being" is negated along with spontaneity and contentment with the present. Life for these individuals centers on what has been or what will be instead of "being." Thus, the very nature of the legal-rational state, by definition of its impositions, is one of malcontent. For corporation and state rule to perpetuate, it must keep the masses under its control as consumers and producers, instilling new wants endlessly (Fromm, 1976).

Never must one be happy with "now." To tolerate the contradictions placed on the self, to tolerate impersonal relations, inauthenticity, and loneliness, the individual places a coating or crust over him/herself. We can see a direct parallel between the characteristics imposed by the structural-situational demands and Goffman's (1959) "dramaturgical" man. The fact that this individual has negated enough of his inner self to successfully handle the frustration of an overrational structure indicates that his humanity has been diminished; he is angry, neurotic, and very lonely. The more fiercely he clings to the rational structure for his life line of ideological security and identity, the more he departs from the true generic social self. Over conformity, compulsive behavior or automotonic behavior is never enough for the rational scheme. He is sapped of his humanity and vitality until his physical capacities give way to stress, disease, and, ultimately, death.

Paradoxically, persons engaged in rationally imputed activity often do not perceive the genesis of their identity loss to be the very structure that promises life eternal, endless security, and, at the very least, a marble stone with their name on it when they are gone. Moreover, they believe the frustration of their self to be inadequacy or the inabiity to cope. Psychologists reinforce such inadequate feelings, dealing with symptoms while ignoring the genesis or pathology of the problem. Their identity also lies within the structure and its maintenance (Becker, 1973).

Where reciprocity and meaningfulness at the generic social level cannot occur because of structural-situational impositions, the person is unable to fit, consider, change, and reconstruct new lines of action with others. The dynamic exchange becomes static; thus the person is isolated or in conflict and without social bonds. Self-concept and identity are also dependent on this reciprocity of action, because the social self takes form and becomes firm as a result of reciprocity of action with others in the process of socialization (Chapman, 1972). The institution of the political state based on this line of reasoning is destroying the social institutions it was designed to cooperatively help survive by altering these structures away from social welfare to power directives.

The institution of economy has as its survival function the production and distribution of goods and services (Young and Mack, 1959). As with the political state, the economic state has been elevated above the other survivial institutions concurrently with the political state. The characteristics of those persons under the imposition of the economic state are substantively the same as with all institutions overrationalized for power and control. Indeed, it behooves man to earn a living through work and gathering the fruits of labor. However, in a rational economic structure persons find acceptable only those rewards that are objective, that is, external to them in terms of material. Self-esteem in this sense lies only in the increased number of "things" we surround ourselves with, not in the quality of such items. Movement out of the needs for survival into the wanting mode of mass production removes persons from the personal self to whichever self the exploiter has in mind. According to Veblen (1963), the emphasis on production and an emphasis is placed on exploitation and robbery of our fellow man. Within this elevated structure, there is no emphasis on "being" but on "having." A person is defined by that which he/she owns. Fromm (1976) describes this nature of having:

> The nature of having mode of existence follows from the nature of private property. In this mode of existence all that matters is my acquisition of property and my unlimited right to keep what I have acquired. The having mode excludes others; it does not require any further effort on my part to keep my property or to make productive use of it. . . In the having mode there is no alive relationship between me and what I have. It and I have become things, and I have it, because I have the force to make it mine. But there is also the reverse relationship: it has me, because my sense of identity, i.e., or sanity, rests upon my having it (and as many things as possible). The having mode of existence is not established by an alive, productive process between subject and object; it makes **things** of both object and subject. The relationship is one of deadness, not of aliveness (pp. 64-65).

The struggle for status, under the conditions imposed by an elevated economic state, moves man away from the generic social level; satisfaction is not found in the internal self but in the external inanimate material with which man surrounds himself. Man is what he possesses-- the car he drives, the clothes he wears, the house he makes payments on, the organizations to which he belongs. Where the object or machine-gadget world dominates the subject in a forced mode of production instead of an "alive production process," both subject and object becomes dead, particularly the subject at the generic social level.

For the construction of reality to exist as a dynamic process between the individual and society, a balance must be sought between the major social institutions so that no one ideology is elevated above any other. The political and economic institutions must be brought into more of a balance at the generic social level with the institutions of religion, school, and the family. By so doing, the characterisitcs imposed on the individual would be maintained at a social level, ecologically sound, economically stable, with decrease domination. Carefully, we must remember that if any institution dominates exploitation will occur. It would be just as falicious to think that the institutions of school or religion or a family should be elevated into a legal-rational order above the Political or Economic Institutions. A balance must be maintained generically, social, and reciprocal. Moreover, science and technology cannot be severed from philosophy, religion, or art, by elevating one form over another. In doing so the content of both is negated. True science cannot negate philosophy nor can true technology negate art (Pirsig, 1974). Science is philosophy, technology is art. Ideology that tears such dual realities apart strikes at the very heart of social man, sequelching the self.

The structural-situational imposition of polarized rational schemes to the negation of "selfhood" persons must come to know for their identity, results in estrangement, and loneliness. How might we then characterize by summary, the person void of self-identity by such impositions? Are there general characteristics of such persons?

Structurally-Situationally Imposed Loneliness

A pattern of general characteristics emerge concerning lonely persons who have been dominated by a structural-situational scheme of overrationalization. In Figure 7 (page 54) antithetical constructs are presented to demonstrate the dual nature of reality, of the mind, and of selfhood. The characteristics listed in the left-hand column represent the polarized constructs imposed on the self to the denial or "ignorance" of the diametric opposition of reality's other half. By imposing these characteristics with particular rewards and punishments to insure their acceptance, the lonely person under such domination will exhibit ideas, beliefs, and behaviors set into and characterized by general overrationalization. The structures rationally elevated have falsely become the social self in its entirety. Specifically, these persons exhibit a self-definition polarized in the following:

1. Rationalism: belief in the logical mathematical, to the exclusion of irrational, aesthetic, religion (generically social), scientism, social Darwinism, man's obtainment of Utopia through the exercise of totality "rationality."

2. Objectification: belief in the measurable, attributing a life and human qualities to the inanimate; worth and value are defined by the accumulation of the "objects" with which they surround themselves.

3. Structural Rigidity: overconforming patterns of work/home affairs; rigid planning of work and leisure time; emphasis on form and appearance; casting images through conspicuous consumption; compulsively neurotic if "things" are not in their place; self-esteem and status are felt by conforming to organizational duty and responsibility even though unethical; emotionless conformity.

4. External Locus of Control: the self is determined by external constraints, structural pressure; conformity in clothing, mannerisms, values transmitted through the imputed media of television, advertising, rationalized indoctrination in school; rationalized churchism.

5. Predictability and Controllability: the self is valued if always consistent and logical; such persons must always be in control of their situation to make it predictable; control of others is their insurance.

6. Mechanistic: quality, a genuine interest in life, leisure, and work are substituted by the consumption of time and material efficiently input and output of materials dominate the quality of the material; number and quantity are of major concern.

7. Objectively Judicial: strict adherence to policy, rules, regulations, and standards; flexibility rests with the person, never in the legal-rational; assumes consensus in law, therefore, law is seen as absolute; objective written law is dominant, not the social significance of the written law.

8. Highly Ordered: bureaucratic structuring in every area of life including the family; the controller in the role of sadist; the controlled in the role of masochist; one-way power imputation from highest in rational "authority" to lowest in "significance;" control of nature; environmental forced into homogeneous material resources; man-made environmental instability.

Loneliness occurs as the self feels something is "missing in life," polarized into the foregoing constructs, but is unable to identify the cause of the anxiety. The constructs that are imposing the polarization of self are the very constructs the people believes or has been led to believe yield true identity of self. Consequently, for the structurally-situationally imposed lonely person, the solution to the anxiety, the contradictions felt, is increased structural form, polarization, and order. Loneliness becomes self-perpetuated once it has been imposed by polarization. What emerges are two sets of factors which perpetuate loneliness: the precipitating factor of polarization by structural-situational imposition; and the maintenance factor of the inability of self to identify the genesis of contradiction clinging to the polarized construct dependently for security. A discussion of these factors will be presented in Chapter V.

Other-Imposed Loneliness

The imposition of loneliness by others, as illustrated in Figure 10 (page 62), places loneliness, a lack of self-identity, in a position with the same direction as the structurally-situationally-imposed self we have previously described. The justification for such a placement at the structural-situational pole lies in the observation that because so many persons are dominated by the structural constructs of over--rationalization and the accompanying characteristics, their impositions in the daily montage of social contacts tend to be not generically social. Such "others" impose their reality constructs upon persons believing them to be their own; but upon further consideration it seems that many of these constructs have only been transferred from the identity constructs of the polarized structural-situational scheme.

What differentiates "other" impositions of self-identity from structural-situational impositions is the cognizance of the source. Persons who impose self-identity constructs in the rational, structural-situational scheme believe and act as if their identity constructs from the "other" mode perceive themselves as their "own person," their own decision maker, their own unique constructor of self. While outwardly demanding they are "masters of their own identity," their values and behavior reveal them as offspring of the polarized construct they do not perceive themselves to be.

This imposition of the "others" on a person is not necessarily the imposing of rational values per se as in the structural, but an insistence on conformity to their particular reality construct. For example, if other persons through peer pressure, chiding, and humiliation impose the behavior of drinking on a person who does not share the same value, the person has a choice of fleeing and disaffiliation, engaging in the "acceptable behavior" as defined by "others," or remaining with others suffering self-isolation within their own minds because they did not engage in drinking. What emerges is the power relationship issuing control by imposition not within a legal-rational structure, but by a person or persons who demand imposing conformity to the group value. The characteristics of the static and asocial power relationships are the same, except we have moved from the general power imposition of legal-rational structures to the particular power impositions of the group or another person. The static nature of power relations has not changed. What has changed are the particular values, beliefs, or behaviors that are imposed. Thus we may observe a counterculture, a group or a person with values, beliefs, and behaviors vastly different from the structural legal-rational values, although the impositions by power directives are carried out in the same manner of persuasion, buying and selling, or coercion.

While the imposition of "self identity" by others may be convincing or accepted they too have placed a "curtain of fantasy" over the dualistic nature of reality to make their lives clear by "absolute" definitions (Ortega, 1957). The fantasy of "absolute" definitions, where a particular aspect of reality's dualism is elevated to a position of dominance, is the same for "others" imposing or the legal-rational imposing. The scope changes, the content (variation) changes, but the form (theme) remains. Kierkegaard (1849) describes the "immediate man" self as:

> . . . his self or he himself is a something included along with 'the other' in the compass of the temporal and the

> worldly . . . Thus the self coheres immediately with 'the other,' wishing, desiring, enjoying, etc. but passively; . . . he manages to imitate the other men, noting how they manage to live, and so he too lives after a sort. In Christendom, he too is a Christian, goes to church every Sunday, hears and understands the parson, yea, they understand one another, he dies; the parson introduces him into eternity for the price of $10--but a self he was not, and a self he did not become. . . For the immediate man does not recognize himself, he recognizes himself only by his dress, . . . he recognizes that he has a self only by externals (p. 184).

Such persons imagime they have an identity if they pay an insurance premium, that they have control of life as they "gun" their sports car, work an electric toothbrush, or ride a motorcycle in a gang.

According to Becker (1973), man has a desire to make his life "heroic." That is, to evolve his own uniqueness out of the apparent confusion external to him. Self-esteem consists of a "hero's welcome" to our self. But the arrival at self is by the destruction of the shell covering the self and facing the anxiety in the terror of existence. Breaking the shell around the self is the realization that to live is to be lost. The more one clings to external imputations of self the more one is lost, for one becomes dependent on a definitions by others rather than his own, concerning self.

The lonely person who finds the imposition of "others" forcing order on his/her chaotic life by the imputation of power directives and not socially reciprocal ones faces a "dilemma of heroism" (Becker, 1973). The lonely choice of conforming to the power directive, where there is order and "other" acceptance, or to choose an alternative nonconformity to the present imputation for some other reality construct is a dilemma.

Within the family though a parent or child may not impose a legal-rational construct of reality on one another, the imposition by power directives of any "absolute" reality construct upon the other or from others results in a dilemma of choice. A loneliness occurs in the self. The more powerful and pervasive the directive the more likely the person is to believe he/she must conform, especially if backed with negative sanctions for nonconformity. Again we see the lack of generic social reciprocity based on power which is necessary for the self to find its identity.

A "loving war" begins as the parent starts to allow a child more independence. With more independence to impose power directives, the child now begins to condemn and criticize the parents. This is particularly true in adolescence. If a formidable amount of care is taken to maintain a generic social bond in early childhood where mutual input to social bonds are allowed, the move through adolescence is less problematic for the child as well as the parents. Instead of being "absolutely" dependent or independent, the self within each family member is aware of and free to bargain for selfhood through interdependency.

Within the schools and churches the imposition of "others" resulting in identity dilemmas may have little to do with values of the structural-situational setting. Instead there may be peer values that are counter to the structural situational. However, the means of imposing an absolute reality construct through power directives is precisely the same, namely, acceptance or rejection by the use of sanctions. To let the self exist as a duality is disallowed: "You are either for me or against me." "Accept me for all I demand of you or reject me and everything I am." But the self within its dilemma to find resolve or to exist dually wants to omit the word "or" from the absolute construct and insert the word "and." "I am for you and I am against you." Being fearful to be so contradictory, the person accepts or rejects another. The expression "you must love me or hate me" forces the self to choose a polarized construct. But is reality "love or hate"? Could not reality be love and hate? This author has observed that the persons one loves the most usually make one the angriest, and the persons one hates the most are usually the persons whose opinions we value more than others; otherwise we would not find them so intimidating. Such "and" constructs of reality are disallowed when reality is elevated to an "either/or" construct by absolute truth ideology.

Within economic and political institutions the impositions by "others" may be aligned with the institution or diametrically opposed to it. A polarization in either direction is deleterious to the social self (Figure 7). Both must exist for survival.

Thus we understand the comparison and contrast of the structural-situational imposition on the self and that imposed by others. The common denominator is the imposition of an absolute polarized reality construct from either extreme of dual reality to the negation of the other possible constructs.

What we must question is not so much the construction of reality but the polarization of the construct by elevating one aspect to the position of total reality. Loneliness decreases in the instant that the duality of self is accepted by the individual and allowed to "be" by others.

Self-Imposed Loneliness

We have examined structural-situational and other impositions of loneliness. The use of power directives and the imputation of a polarized construct of reality, as has been demonstrated, results in the loss of self-identity, alienation and loneliness. Let us now examine the person who imposes loneliness upon him/herself; a better term may be aloneness. It must be remembered that physical isolation from others and the structure of institutions may not be lonely at all, but a chance to give the self's duality a time to exist unhampered by power directives and polar reality constructs.

Many assume that a lack of contact with other persons, definitionally, is loneliness (Gordon, 1976). This is particulary true in some theories about the aged (i.e., disengagement theory). However, a recent study (Rubenstein, Shaver, and Peplau, 1979) suggest that the elderly may be the least likely to be lonely. They may find more contentment with self because of the reduction of legal-rational imputation after they are retired. This too would vary based on the degree of acceptance of the polarized legal-rational construct as the "total reality" during a process of employment. Some of the elderly may feel emotionally and physically isolated, particularly if they accepted the work place, monetary rewards, and the structural arrangements of legal-rational systems as definitional of success and self esteem. Others may see retirement as an opportunity to "find themselves" once again.

The persons who are alone and lonely may be in this position because of structural and other impositions. They do not desire to be alone and lonely but have been externally battered into this condition. This would suggest loneliness by imposition of the two types already discussed.

Self-imposed aloneness, without self-feelings of loneliness, becomes a positive experience for the person imposing this condition upon him/herself. Earlier we discussed the "dilemma of heroism." Aloneness can be seen as a reaction to external impositions of selfhood. There are many examples of music, art, and literature that indicate that the creative withdrew into physical isolation for self-reflection. The heroism involved in such behavior seems not one of external definitions of self-esteem but one of internal self-actualizing (Maslow, 1954). But the creative endeavor while in aloneness is usually produced for the esteem of others in the form of a book, work of art, or a selection of music as its final goal. That is, an "object" of approval or disapproval for others to judge, though approval may only come after the creator's death, (i.e. Mark Twain, Van Gogh).

What differentiates self-imposed aloneness from loneliness imposed by others and the structural-situational is the person's awareness of their unique existence. These individuals have moved back to examine themselves and the external "selves" or roles they have been expected to play. What makes aloneness in this respect so positive to self-identity is not the outcome or productive object for others to grade and assess, but the creative process itself. In such moments of aloneness, self-reflection, and mental debate, the person becomes increasingly aware of him/herself as <u>created</u> by the environment and <u>creator</u> of that environment. There is self-satisfaction and immeasurable freedom in such a notion. Oneself can "be" what one wishes oneself to "be." Such ideas are labeled by the structural-situational and others as delusional, madness, and deviance. "Creativity of the self" is a nice expression for madness if one's definition of normal is polarized in legal-rational constructs which discourage creativity, new thought, and change.

Such aloneness is not without problems. One may polarize into any possible reality construct and decide it to be the whole of reality. For example, in the case of extreme subjectivism, impulsiveness, or other "contents" void of "form," Becker (1973) explains:

> The key to the creative type is that he is separated out of the common pool of shared meanings. There is something in his life experience that makes him take the world as a problem; as a result he has to make personal sense out of it . . . Existence becomes a problem that needs an ideal answer; but when you no longer accept the collective

solution to the problem of existence, then you must fashion your own. The work of art is, then, the ideal answer of the creative type to the problem of existence as he takes it in--not only the existence of the external world, but especially his own: who he is as a painfully separate person with nothing shared to lean on. He has to answer to his extreme individuation, his so painful isolation (p. 171).

The self-imposition of aloneness may have positive and negative consequences for the person who seeks to believe in his/her "own private religion." Depending on the intensity of the self-imposition and length of time, the person may be considered as an artist if definitions by "others" and the structural demands are approving of the object/product; or they may be considered mad if external impositions show disapproval. Sometimes it is difficult to define an action or object as the work of a genius or a madman. What defines it as good or bad is appraisal from others. This ideal plagues physicians of institutions for the mentally ill; they have become keenly aware that some persons are institutionalized not because they could not live with society, but because society and more "normal" persons could not live with them.

Extreme individuation in the mind and physical surroundings becomes as polarized as the polarized constructs imposed by "others" and the structural-situational. Though the elevated construct may be different, the same dependency and acceptance of a polarized construct as "whole reality" occurs nonetheless. Drawing oneself away into physical isolation may help as a creative endeavor but may also deny others of one's presence for mutual interaction, particularly family members and friends. This too denies the generic social bond, one of mutual interdependence and reciprocity, to exist. The dynamic duality of selfhood is denied by elevating a polarized static construct of reality to the level of "total" reality.

Summary

In each of our typologies of loneliness (structurally-situationally-imposed, other-imposed, and self imposed) the dominant feature is the polarization of a particular reality construct as "total" reality to the negation of other possible constructs. The dual self is negated when it is compelled to follow "either/or" constructs and not "both." Watts

(1972) has called this the game of "Black-and-White." For loneliness to decrease by allowing the dual self to think and behave, a realization must be made that:

> so-called opposites such as light and darkness, and sound and silence, solid and space, on and off, inside and outside, appearing and disappearing, cause and effect, are poles or aspects of the same thing. But we have no word for the thing, save such vague concepts as Existence, Being, God, or the Ultimate Ground for Being (p. 30).

As the author ponders the question of loneliness, what becomes apparent is that the more a person polarizes into "either/or" constructions of reality the farther selfhood, self-identity, self-dualism are torn apart. Existence is fragmented. Ideally, the generic social self would be equally influenced by the structural-situational, others, and self (Figure 12). In describing the three categories of impositions placed on the person or by the person, this author by design focused more heavily on the structural-situational impositions of the reality construct and loneliness than on the other two types. This was done because the impositions by structural-situational variables by society have changed,

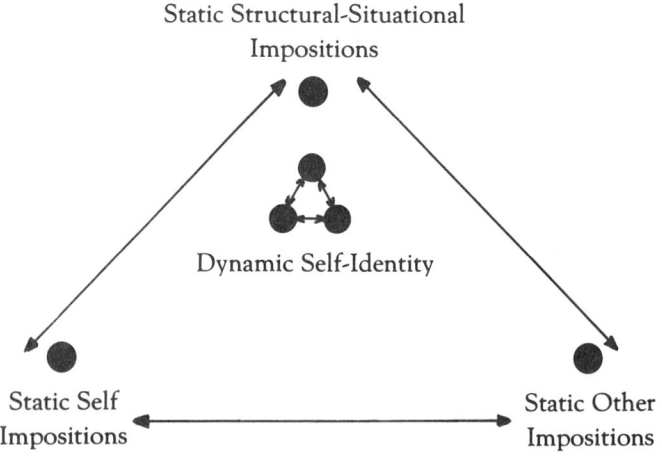

Figure 12: **Equidistant Adherence to All Reality Constructs and Placement of the Dual Generic Social Self**

particularly in the past 100 to 200 years (Figure 13). Figure 13 represents more adequately the relationship between the three impositions of reality constructs than was presented in Figure 10 (page 62). For generic dual selfhood and identity to be increased, and loneliness, alienation, and isolation to be decreased, a balance in the middle of all possible reality constructions must be maintained. The notion is implied that reality is dynamic and relative, not static and absolute. The ideal positioning of persons should be allowance for selfhood, self-identity, and the dualism of self. Represented is the ideal dual self in the center; the other models represent a shift to polar constructs. The hollow circle represents the negated aspects of reality.

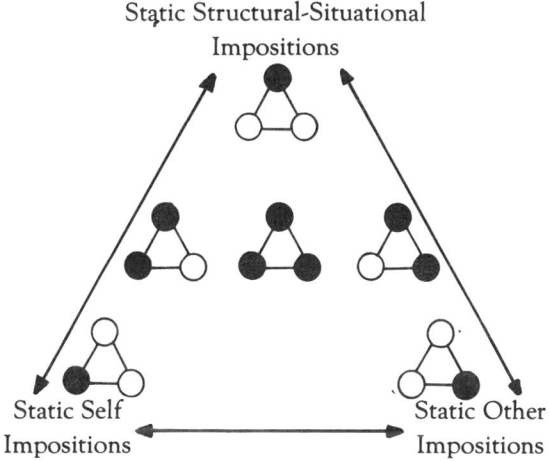

Figure 13: Unequal Adherence by Imposition to Polarized Constructs and the Placement of the Asocial Fragmented Self

Thus far we have traced society through change into the present reality construction imposed by legal-rational schemes upon the self. It is not possible, by maintaining this path of reasoning, to construct a model for loneliness based on the move away from generic socially-derived constructs of reality to imposed polarized constructs of reality.

Chapter V will discuss the loneliness model and the specific variables which determine its magnitude and intensity.

CHAPTER V

THE THEORETICAL MODEL OF LONELINESS

Presented in Chapter IV was the case for loneliness as an imbalance of reality construction between structural-situational impositions, imposition of others, and imposition by the individual self. Because the "contruction of reality" is an abstract term, it is not easily quantified or measured. Nonetheless, we can create categories of loneliness based on the imposition of reality constructs which are measurable, though the variables are not completely discrete and some overlap may occur. As shown in Figure 12 and 13, the various constructs and dynamics between constructs can vary for each person, depending on the magnitude and intensity of the polarized imposition.

Each dynamic position represented in Figure 13 can be given a numerical value shown in Figure 14. The assignment of numerical values to the possible reality constructs corresponds to the number of polarized positions negated by the elevation of one or more positions as "total" reality. Thus, if only the structural-situational is elevated while self and other impositions are negated, the value of –2 is representative of the distance from the center position, which is a dynamically constructed reality. The farther the person moves from the center (+3), the more imbalanced the self identity becomes. Polarization toward any of the three modes of reality construction increases the intensity of selflessness.

Within such a model (Figure 14) there can be no one absolute point to place a person, for each mental construction of reality may differ infinitely between rational-irrational, form-content, and structural-situational-other self imputations, just as there are perpetual shifts possible in self identity concepts. Nonetheless, as a general mode of reality construction and polarization of the construction, the model can be considered representative. It is acknowledged that this model is symbolic and cannot totally depict reality. It is used only for <u>descriptive</u> purposes and <u>explanation</u>.

The person least likely to suffer from loneliness, alienation, and selflessness (perhaps a better term is self-myopia) is the person who is able to balance dynamically in the middle of the possible ranges of reality construction. Instead of considering only one particular facet of

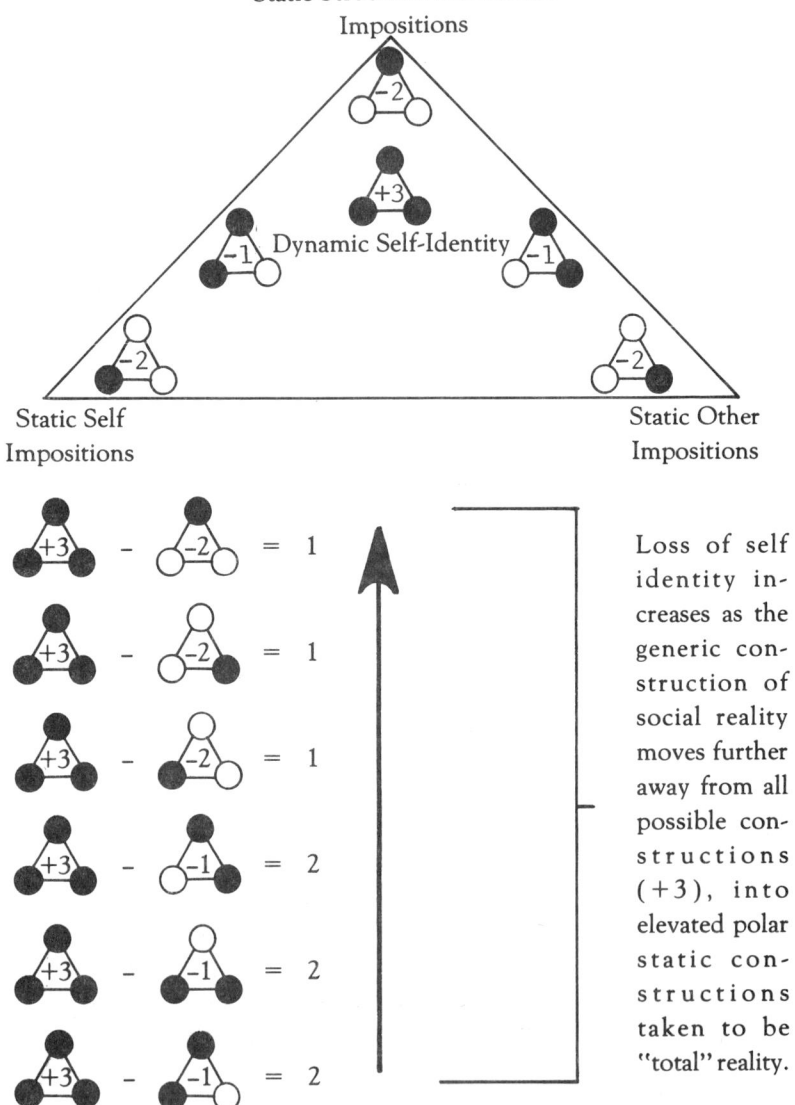

Figure 14. Static Structural-Situational Impositions

reality, such persons are able to understand the multi-faceted nature of reality construction. This does necessarily indicate that any perspective of reality could be as equally right as it is wrong. This seems to be an insecure position to take concerning reality. It would be more secure to particularize to an absolute, adhering to it adamantly. But there is a great deal of security in understanding dynamic reality as opposed to control of and adherence to a static particular reality. The reductionism involved in particularizing "total" reality brings not understanding but subjugation to the partial reality construct and to others similarly subjugated (Chapman, 1971). As movement into "particular outlooks" occurs, freedom of inquiry, freedom of self, and freedom of selfhood are reduced to subjugation and control. As movement from the dynamic self-identity (Figure 14) occurs, part of the self is negated, which is "a psychosis that has advanced far in the present thought forms of the world" (Chapman, 1971).

The interaction between imposition types of loneliness depicted in the model serves as a general description of possible modalities which produce the loss of self. More specifically is the interaction within each polar type which affects the length, magnitude, and intensity of the lonely self.

Interaction Within Component Impositions of Loneliness

Persons who have polarized in any direction away from dynamic self-identity, because of imposition of the structural-situational, other, and self, may describe their existence as lonely, isolated, alienated, and anomic. But what are the variables or influences that maintain a person in a rigid construction of reality which make self-identity, acceptance, and selfhood difficult to grasp? Whether persons can move away from a polarized static construction of reality into a generically dynamic construction of reality is dependent on the person's ability to identify the following:

1. The locus of control or causality (internal and external).

2. Stability or length of time one has been polarized into a static reality construct.

3. Controllability--does the person perceive his/her self as having any control to affect change?

4. The separation of the polar reality constructs that imposed loneliness and the reality constructs that are maintaining the person in the polarized static reality.

Locus of Control or Causality

Persons who feel an imposition on the self--the structural-situational, other, or self by way of reaction to external constraints--may or may be able to identify the genesis of the problem. For example, if the "organizational man" (Whyte, 1956) has been overwhelmed by the imposition of the structural-situational rationalism and bureaucratization, he may identify the loss of self. But he may strive to conform compulsively and increase the organization of his existence. He does not realise that as he increases his conformity to the structural-situational reality construct, he is insuring the further polarization of his self. In striving for balance (dynamic self-identity) he moves into an imbalance (static selflessness). Conversely, if a person recognized the rationalism and bureaucratization of the structural-situational impositions as the locus of control, he may soon realize that to maintain a balanced self he must offset the influence of this static construction of reality with its polar opposite (i.e., spontaneity, aesthetics, art, music, and creativity), thereby moving the construction of reality toward the middle dynamic position (Figure 14).

The imposition of reality constructs that have been polarized by others and self are similarly identified. Persons may ask, "I am lonely, out of touch with my self; is it because of my situation, because of others, or because I have chosen this myself?" Whichever of the three polar constructs has been elevated to dominance in the person's construction of reality must be offset by the missing infuence of the other negated construct(s) in order to maintain the balanced dynamic self-identity. If the imposition by the structural-situational, others, or self demands the person adhere to no other possible reality construction, the person then has reason to be suspicious of the truth and rightness of the construct. The identification of the locus of control is difficult. A slave strives to gain freedom; a master strives to insure slavery. Thus it is an onerous task for the lonely person to identify the genesis of the feelings of loneliness. Finding one's self is a gloomy journey away from the security of a preconstructed polar reality in which one has been "pigeon-holed." Even though a person realizes that "something inside is not right," the fear of traveling to selfhood, becoming dynamic, becoming form and content, becoming fluid in the movement from subject to object and object to subject is too alarming a proposition.

Those persons who identify the genesis of their selflessness as one of the three impositions (Figure 14) have a chance to reckom with and change the construction of their "selves." But even among these persons who identify the genesis of loneliness are those who prefer, as Watts (1970) terms it, "ignor"ance. Many of us have encountered individuals who are, by every external standard, "successful," "educated," and "well to do" but are "ignor"ant. Therefore, we see that even the identification of the locus of control or causality of selfless reality constructs does not insure the movement out of such constructs.

Stability of Polar Constructions of Reality

Another important element in the dynamic of reality constructions, polarization, and loneliness (selflessness) is the stability or amount of time a person has been locked into a static polar reality construction. The longer the person remains in the static construct, the more difficult it becomes for the person to free him/herself of its imposition. The dependency on the static construct is much the same as an addiction to anything. Slater (1978) in his book Wealth Addiction, has as well described the addiction to wealth as the same as any other addiction, even to the point of having withdrawal symptoms.

Controllability of Selflessness

Whether the person who experience feelings of loneliness (selflessness) continues to grasp the static reality constructs, that have negated the rest of the "self" is dependent on the person's perception of controllability. If the person believes his/her selflessness, as imposed by the structural-situational, others, and self, is out of his/her control, he/she will cling more desperately to the imposed construct, moving him/her farther away from the dynamic self-identity. What college professor has suggested a new idea opposed to the present society notions and has heard students remark, "It's an interesting idea, but it will never work; the world just isn't that way." This indicates that there exists a classroom of polar reality constructors. When asking the same students "How is the world?" tension shows on most of the faces.

Though the students are "absolute" in saying "this is the way the world is," they are "unabsolute" and disagree when each tries to explain that "is" means. The same dilemma exists for any number of persons who have polarized their reality constructs to the "ignor"ance and negation of any other construct, regardless of occupation.

Conversely, persons may perceive their "selves" as having control over the reality-ruts into which they have fallen. These persons are able to avoid the static reality ruts and move through many constructions of reality with relative ease. It requires courage to move out of the rigidly imposed reality constructs of the structural-situational, of others, and of self to examine the infinite range of reality constructs. It may cost a job, a car, or a house, but these have no meaning if one obtains them and disallows the self to search for itself.

> For what is a man profited, if he shall gain the whole world, and lose his own soul (self) or what shall a man give in exchange for his soul (self) (King James Bible, Matthew 16, verse 26)?

The longer the person polarizes reality constructs, the more impossible it becomes to consider other possible constructs. They have been too long negated. Thus the saint condemns the sinner; the bureaucrat condemns the bohemian; and the scientist condemns the artist. In group-out group relationships are based on the particular group's static construct of reality; hence they attempt to elevate one construct of reality above the others as 'rightly more valid." The awareness that each construct of reality is as validly part of the whole reality as any other is forgotten.

How particularized the person becomes in a myopic construct of reality and the stability or the length of time they are plagued with this myopia influences how far removed from the "self", which is dual in nature, that the person has become.

Loneliness, selflessness, will decrease at the point in which the person becomes intensely aware, understanding the multi-reality construction of the whole reality. Afterall there are saintly sinners and sinning saints, bureaucratic bohemians and bohemian bureaucrats, and scientific artists as well as artistic scientists (Pirsig, 1974). The stagnation in a particular reality construct, with time, becomes permanent "social death" (Chapman, 1971).

The identification of the selfless, lonely person must include as a dimension the length of time the person has been in a static reality-rut. How many persons in modern society find themselves in a rut and of those how many are lonely? The rut can only be avoided by continually changing as one engages in generically social interaction, allowing for generically social constructions of reality.

How well a person perceives his/her self as having control to effect change within his/her own existence will increase or decrease the persistence of selflessness. This is indicated by persons who are lonely, using words such as lost, out of control, desperate, frightened, without being able to identify the genesis of these feelings. It is the dual self within these persons to revolt, frustrated by the imposition of a single self-construct as "the total self." The dual self responds with feelings of being hopelessly out of control.

Precipitation and Maintenance of Loneliness

We have discussed locus of control, stability, and controllability of loneliness as a condition of selflessness to better understand the within interaction of the general model presented in Figure 14. These three dimensions are present as a person seeks to sort out the precipitating events, situations, or behaviors that affect loneliness. However, persons are able to do this only insofar as they identified the locus of control, that the duration of the selflessness is not great, and that the move back toward the dynamic self-identity (Figure 14) is in their control. If the person is aware of these elements, understands the duality of the self, and reduces the imposition of precipitated and maintained aspects of loneliness, then a shift can be made to a multi-dimensional reality construct. For example, a person may identify a major event in the structural-situational, with others, or with self as the imposed precipitate of loneliness, but the resulting imbalance in reality constructs may cause the maintenance of attributes of withdrawal, hopelessness, feelings of emptiness, isolation, and alienation. To maintain or polarize into such attributes as a reaction to the imposed reality constructs is to be dependent on static constructs which if perpetuated causes one to sink further into selflessness.

CHAPTER VI

CONCLUSIONS

The feelings of loneliness and the search for self-identity which man has sought to reconcile throughout history continue to be present. If the discrepancy between man's ideal dynamic self-identity and the static imposed constructions of reality are too great, feelings of selflessness will dominate man's existence.

Through the elevated rational schemes of social Darwinism and evolutionary development to a planned Utopia, society has changed, continually negating the dynamic self. This negation is an effort to bring power, control, and dominance over individuals. Imposition of a rational scheme elevated into "total" reality negates the self of the infinitely changing construction of reality. To elevate a snap-shot photographic construction of reality as the only reality construct is to negate the dynamic moving picture of generic social interaction. The self requires perpetual reciprocity with others and things to continue its movement as a dynamic social entity. When movement and reciprocity are stifled by particularistic reality constructs that are taken to be "total" reality, the aspects of the self which do not fit are dismissed as nonexistent. But the self is socially dynamic and is not fooled by the imposed constructions of reality from the structural-situational, from others, and from the person. The self not being fooled reacts with anxiety, fear, loneliness, and alienation, though it may not be able to precisely identify the genesis of those feelings.

As long as one person imposes a static construction of reality for control over another person or group, the dynamic self will feel the contradiction between a power-directed reality construction and its dynamic construction of reality. It is this difference in the dynamic "self's" desired existence and the actual imposed existence that makes loneliness a continual problem.

A discrepancy in a person's desired life and actual life is basic to the conflicts and social problems that exist. It is in this respect that loneliness is symptomatic of imposed reality constructs by a power structure, as is poverty, racism, and class conflict (Marx, 1867). The pervasiveness of loneliness is as socially problematic as any other aspect of society that grew in intensity with the social change of industrialization, bureaucratization, and secularization. If Sorokin (1941) was correct, society should begin to shift back toward the ideational, away from the now sensate forms of the static reality construction. If society and culture move in this direction, perhaps he can maintain the relative ideal between the polar extremes. Authors such as Fromm (1976), Reich (1970), and Watts (1966, 1968) believe the move is occurring presently toward a new consciousness. By depolarizing reality constructs we may experience a decline in the number of persons with feelings of selflessness. The interrelationships of societies and ideologies are complex; but if compared to the human minds that have created them, they are simple. The self of man must be allowed to continue reciprocally in the infinite ways it constructs reality. If the self of man is not allowed to maintain its dynamics because of lesser imputed elevated constructions of reality imposed for power, the self and man will not survive. If the institutions that were designed to insure survival rigidly impose a distorted reality on man, the institutions will be the cause of death and not survival. When there are no socially dynamic persons existing, the institutions will have destroyed themselves.

For the self to find itself and maintain its duality, it must continually seek paths of reality constructions which are out of the mainstream of the imposed constructions. The person in search of self must have the courage to wind down the "Road Not Taken" (Frost, 1916:

> Two roads diverged in a yellow wood,
> And sorry I could not travel both
> And be one traveler, long I stood
> And looked down one as far as I could
> To where it bent in the undergrowth;
>
> Then took the other, as just as fair,
> And having perhaps the better claim,
> Because it was grassy and wanted wear;
> Though as for that the passing there
> Had worn them really about the same,

And both that morning equally lay
In leaves no step had trodden black.
Oh, I kept the first for another day!
Yet knowing how way leads on the way,
I doubted if I should ever come back.

I shall be telling this with a sigh
Somewhere ages and ages hence:
Two roads diverged in a wood, and I--
I took the one less traveled by,
And that has made all the difference.

Loneliness and selflessness of a fragmented dynamic self by power impositions must be avoided or man will cease to exist. It is the responsibility of each individual to understand and acknowledge the multiple constructions of reality in those they encounter so that the "happenings" of life may continue to be serious and humorous, saintly and sinful, mystical and practical, and competitive and cooperative, with the "happening" of the self remaining alive and well.

BIBLIOGRAPHY

Articles

Acuff, G., and D. Allen
    1970   "Hiatus in Meaning: Disengagement for Retired Professors." *Journal of Gerontology.* Vol. 25, No. 2, pp. 126-128.

Anderson, I.
    1970   "Wind up," taken from *Jethro Tull Aqualung*, Los Angeles Chrysalis Records.

Bowman, C.
    1955   "Loneliness and Social Change." *American Journal of Psychiatry,* 112, 194-198.

Carlyle, T.
    1829   "Signs of the times" in A. Shelston (ed) Thomas Carlyle: Selected Writings (Penguin Books, 1971) pp. 65-67.

Domhoff, G. W.
    1974   "State and ruling class in corporate America." *The Insurgent Sociologist,* 5, Spring: 3-16.

Fromm-Reichmann, F.
    1959   "Loneliness." *Psychiatry,* 22, pp. 1-15.

Frost, R.
    1916   "The road not taken" from *Complete Poems of Robert Frost,* Holt Rinehart and Winston, Inc., New York, p. 18.

Gerth, H. J. and C. Wright Mills
    1958   "From Max Weber: Essays in Sociology." New York: Oxford University Press.

Glick, P. and A. Norton
    1977   "Marrying, divorcing, and living together in the U.S. today." *Population Reference Bureau,* Vol. 12, No. 5, October.

Hardin, G.
    1968   "The tragedy of the commons." *Science,* 162: 1243-1248.

Horton, J.
    1966   "Order and Conflict Theories of Social Problems as Competing Ideologies." Vol. 71 #6 *American Journal of Sociology,* pp. 701-713.

Hynson, L.M.
1979 "Divorce, widowhood, and satisfaction with health status for men and women. *Free Inquiry*, Vol. 7, No. 2, November.

Jackings, H.
1976 "The theory of liberation," in *Rough Notes from Liberation I and II* (Seattle: Rational Island Publishers).

Kolakowski, L.
1977 "Marxist roots of Stalinism" in Robert C. Tucker, editor, *Stalinism, Essays in Historical Interpretation*, New York: W. W. Norton, 283-298.

Laslett, P.
1960 "The sovereignty of the family." *The Listener*, April. 7.

Leopold, A.
1949 "The land ethic." An essay in a *Sand County Almanac*: New York, Oxford University Press.

Little, J.
1964 "I care, you care, he cares." *Harpers Magazine*, 1964.

Lowenthal, M.F.
1964 "Social isolation and mental illness in old age." *American Sociological Review*, Vol. 29, No. 1, February.

Mead, G. H.
1912 "The Mechanisms of Social Conciousness." *Journal of Philosophy*, 9: 401-406.

Meltzer, B.N.
1964 "Meads social psychology." From the *Social Psychology of George Herbert Mead*, pp. 10-31. Center for Sociological Research, Western Michigan University.

Peppers, L. G. and R. J. Knapp
1980 "Life satisfaction and attitudes toward death. *Free Inquiry*, Vol. 8, No. 1, May.

Rubenstein, C., P. Shaver, and L. A. Peplau
1979 "Loneliness." *Human Nature*, Vol. 2, Number 2.

Schweitzer, Albert
1923 "Die schuldder philosophic an dem niedergang der kultur (The responsibility of philosophy for the decay of culture). *Gesammelte Werke*, Vol. 2, Zurich: Bachclub Ex Libris.

Seeman, M.
1975 "Alienation studies." In A Inkeles (ed) *Annual Review of Sociology*: Palo Alto, California.

U.S. Bureau of the Census
   1976   "Household and family characteristics." *Current Population Reports.* Series p. 20, No. 311. Washington, D.C.: U.S. Government Printing Office, 1977.

Whorf, B. L.
   1952   "Language, mind and reality." A *Review of General Semantics,* Vol. IX, No. 3 (Spring). p. 181.

Books

Arendt, H.
   1951   *The Origins of Totalitarianism.* New York. Harcount, Brace and World.

Bach, G. R., and H. Goldberg
   1975   *"Creative Aggression: The Art of Assertive Living.* New York: Avon Books.

Barrett, W.
   1958   *Irrational Man: A Study in Existential Philosophy.* Doubleday and Company, Inc.

Becker, C.
   1932   *The Heavenly City of the Eighteenth Century Philosophers.* New Haven.

Becker, E.
   1973   *The Denial of Death.* The Free Press, Macmillan Publishers, New York.

Berne, E.
   1961   *Transactional Analysis in Psychotherapy.* New York: Grove Press.

Bower, S. A. and G. H. Bower
   1976   *Asserting Yourself.* Reading Mass.: Addison-Wesley.

Bowlby, J.
   1973   *Attachment and Loss.* Vol. II, Separation: Anxiety and Anger. New York: Basic Books.

Brinton, C.
   1960   *The Shaping of the Modern Mind.* Menton Books, The New American Library.

Brittan, A.
   1973   *Meanings and Situations.* London: Routledge and Degal Paul.

Burns, T.
1969 *Industrial Man.* Penguin Books.
Caine, L.
1974 *Window.* New York: William Morrow and Co.
Caine, L.
1978 *Lifeliness.* Garden City, New York: Doubleday and Co.
Chapman, I.
1971 *The End of Free Inquiry: A Study in Reality Construction.* Published by Ivan Chapman, Oklahoma State University.
Chapman, I.
1972 *Maintenance of Societal Thresholds: A Social Imperative.* Published by Ivan Chapman, Oklahoma State University.
Cooley, C. H.
1902 *Human Nature and the Societal Order.* New York: Scribner and Sons.
Cooley, C. H.
1909 *Social Organization.* New York: Charles Scribners Sons.
Cuzzort, R. R.
1969 *Humanity and Modern Sociological Thought.* New York: Holt, Rinehart, and Winston.
Dyer, W.
1978 *Pulling Your Own Strings.* New York: Funk and Wagnalls.
Eitzen, E. S.
1974 *Social Structure and Social Problems.* Allyn and Bacon, Inc., Boston.
Feilinghetti, L.
1958 *A Coney Island of the Mind.* New York: New Directions Publishing Company.
Frankl, V. E.
1963 *Man's Search For Meaning.* New York: Washington Square Press.
Fromm, E.
1941 *Escape From Freedom.* New York: Rinehart and Company.
Fromm, E.
1955 *The Sane Society.* Holt, Rinehart, Winston, Inc., New York.
Fromm, E.
1976 *To Have Or To Be.* Bantam Books, Harper and Row Publishers, New York.

Goffman, E.
   1959   *The Presentation of Self in Everyday Life.* Garden City, New Jersey: Doubleday.

Gordon, S.
   1976   *Lonely in America.* Touchstone Books, Simon and Schuster, New York.

Gouldner, A.
   1970   *The Coming Crisis in Western Sociology.* New York: Basic Books.

Halmos, P.
   1952   *Solitude and Privacy.* Philosophical Library, Routledge and Kegan-Paul, Ltd.

Hill, S.
   1979   *Demystifying Social Deviance.* New York: McGraw-Hill.

Horkheimer, Max
   1936   *Psychologic Der Autoritat in Autoritat Und Familie.* Alcan, Paris.

Horney, Karen
   1936   *The Neurotic Personality of Our Time.* W. W. Norton and Company, New York.

Howard, J. A.
   1975   *The Flesh-Colored Cage.* New York: Hawthorn Books.

Hunt, M. and B. Hunt
   1977   *The Divorce Experience.* New York: McGraw-Hill.

Jameson, M. C.
   1970   *A Bill of Rights for Kids.* Englewood Cliffs, New Jersey: Prentice-Hall.

Johnson, S. M.
   1977   *First Person Singular: Living the Good Life Alone.* New York: Lippincott.

Jung, C. G.
   1955   *Modern Man in Search of A Soul.* Translated by W. S. Dell and Cary F. Baynes. New York: Harvest Books, Harcount, Brace, and World.

Kenniston, K.
   1960   *Alienation and the Decline of Utopia.* American Scholar, Spring.

Kierkegaard, Soren
    1844   *The Concept of Dread*. Princeton: University Press, edition, 1957, translated by Walter Lowrie.

Kierkegaard, Soren
    1849   *The Sickness Unto Death*. (Anchor edition, 1954, translated by Walter Lowrie.) Anchor Books, New York.

Kornhauser, W.
    1959   *The Politics of Mass Society*. Glencoe Illinois: Free Press.

Kumar, K.
    1978   *Prophesy and Progress*. Penguin Books, Ltd. Harmondsworth, Middlesex, England.

Lauer, R.
    1973   *Perspectives on Social Change*. Boston: Allyn and Bacon, Inc.

Linton, R.
    1936   *The Study of Man*. New York: Appleton-Century-Crofts, Inc.

Marcuse, H.
    1964   *One Dimensional Man*. Beacon Press, Boston.

Martin, D.
    1978   *A General Theory of Secularization*. New York: Harper and Row Publishers.

Marx, K.
    1867   *Das Capital*. (Translated by Eden and Cedar Paul in two volumes, Everyman edition, J. M. Dent and Sons, 1930.)

Maslow, A. H.
    1954   *Motivation and Personality*. New York: Harper and Row, 1954.

Matthew, 16:26
    King James Version, *The Holy Bible*, published by Command of King James, England.

May, R., E. Angel, and H. F. Ellenberger
    1958   *Existence--A New Dimension in Psychiatry and Psychology*. New York: Basic Books, Inc.

McGinnis, J.
    1968   *The Selling of the President*. New York: Random.

Meneken, H. L.
    1963   *Man's Search for Meaning*. New York: Washington Square Press.

Miller, A. R.
    1971   *Assault on Privacy.* New York: Menton Book, New American Library.

Miller, S.
    1963   *The Dilemma of Modern Belief.* New York: Harper and Row.

Mills, C. W.
    1956   *The Power Elite.* Oxford University Press. Oxford, England.

Mills, C. W.
    1959   *The Sociological Imagination.* New York: Oxford University Press.

Moore, W.
    1962   *The Attributes of An Industrial Order.* in S. Nosow and W. H. Form (eds.) *Man, Work and Society,* (Atherton, New York).

Morris, D.
    1971   *Intimate Behavior.* New York: Random House.

Moustakas, C. E.
    1961   *Loneliness.* New York: Random House.

Moustakas, C. E.
    1972   *Loneliness and Love.* Englewood Cliffs, New Jersey: Prentice-Hall.

Moustakas, C. E.
    1975   *Portraits of Loneliness and Love.* Englewood Cliffs, New Jersey: Prentice-Hall.

Mumford, L.
    1937   *Technics and Civilization.* Harcourt, Brace, and World, Inc.

Nisbet, R.
    1953   *The Quest for Community.* New York: Oxford University Press.

Ogburn, W. F.
    1922   *Social Change.* New York: B. W. Huebseh, Inc.

Ortega, Jose
    1957   *The Revolt of the Masses.* New York: Norton.

Packard, V.
    1972   *A Nation of Strangers.* New York: David McKay, Inc.

Park, R. E.
    1950   *Race and Culture.* New York: Knickerbocker Printing Corporation.

Parsons, T.
    1951   *The Social System.* New York: Free Press.

Pirsig, R. M.
   1974   *Zen and the Art of Motorcycle Maintenance.* New York: Bantam Books, Wiliam Morrow and Company.

Quinney, R.
   1980   *Class, State, and Crime.* Longman, Inc, New York.

Reich, C. A.
   1970   *The Greening of America.* New York: Bantam Books, Random House, Inc.

Reich, Wilhelm
   1933   *Charakteranalyse.* Wien, 1933.

Reisman, D., R. Denny, and N. Glazer
   1961   *The Lonely Crowd.* New Haven, Connecticut: Yale University Press.

Robinson, E. A.
   1956   *The Town Down the River and the Children of the Night.* Boston, Massachusetts: Charles Scribner's Sons.

Rodale, R.
   1972   *Ecology and Luxury Living May Not Mix.* Emmaus, Pennsylvania: Rodale Press.

Roszak, T.
   1973   *Where the Wasteland Ends.* New York: Doubleday, Anchor.

Schrag, P.
   1978   *Mind Control.* New York: Dell Publishing Company.

Shanas, E.
   1968   *Old People in Three Industrial Societies.* New York: Atherton Press.

Silberman, C. E.
   1970   *Crisis in the Classroom: The Remaking of American Education.* New York: Random House.

Simmel, G.
   1950   *The Sociology of George Simmel.* Glencoe, Illinois: Free Press.

Slater, P.
   1970   *The Pursuit of Loneliness.* Boston: Beacon Press.

Sorokin, P. A.
   1941   *The Crisis of Our Age.* New York: Dutton Press.

Spann, J. R.
   1950   *The Christian Faith and Secularism.* Nashville: Abington-Cokesbury Press.

Stonequist, E. V.
   1937   *The Marginal Man: A Study in Personality and Culture Conflict.* New York: Russell and Russell.

Sullivan, H. S.
   1953   *The Interpersonal Theory of Psychiatry.* New York: W. W. Norton and Company.

Sumner, W. G.
   1906   *Folkways.* Boston.

Sweet, W.
   1948   *The Story of Religion in America.*

Tanner, I.
   1973   *Loneliness: The Fear of Love.* New York: Harper and Row, Publishers.

Tillich, P.
   1948   *The Protestant Era.* Chicago: University of Chicago Press.

Tillich, P.
   1963   *The Eternal Now.* New York: Charles Scribner's Sons.

Toennies, F.
   1957   *Community and Society.* New York: Harper and Row Publishers.

Turner, J. and L. Beeghley
   1981   *The Emergence of Sociological Theory.* Dorsey Press, Homewood, Illinois.

Urick, R.
   1970   *Alienation: Individual or Social Problem.* Englewood Cliffs, New Jersey: Prentice-Hall.

Veblen, Thorstein
   1963   *The Theory of the Leisure Class.* New York: A Mentor Book, Published by The New American Library.

Watts, A.
   1972   *On the Taboo Against Knowing Who You Are.* New York: Random House.

Weber, M.
   1922   *The Three Types of Legitimate Rule.* Translated by Hans Gerth. Berkeley Journal of Sociology, 1953.

Weber, M.
   1947   *The Theory of Social and Economic Organization.* Translated by A. M. Henderson and Talcott Parsons (New York: The Free Press).

Weiss, R. S.
   1973   *Loneliness: The Experience of Emotional and Social Isolation.* Cambridge: MIT Press.

Whyte, W.
   1956   *The Organization Man.* Simon and Schuster, New York.

Wolfe, T.
   1935   *The Hills Beyond.* New York: Harper and Bros.

Wolfe, T.
   1976   *Theme Decade and the Third Great Awakening.* New York: Farrar, Straus, and Grioux.

Wrong, D.
   1979   *Power: Its Forms, Bases, and Uses.* New York: Harper and Row Publishers.

Wydro, K.
   1978   *Flying Solo: The New Art of Living Single.* New York: Berkeley Publishing Company.

Young, K. and Raymond Mack
   1959   *Sociology and Social Life.* New York: American Book Company.

Zimbardo, P.
   1977   *Shyness.* Reading, Massachusetts: Addison-Wesley.